WALCH PUBLISHING

Daily Warm-Ups

WORLD GEOGRAPHY & CULTURES

Kate O'Halloran

Level II

The classroom teacher may reproduce materials in this book for classroom use only.
The reproduction of any part for an entire school or school system is strictly prohibited.
No part of this publication may be transmitted, stored, or recorded in any form
without written permission from the publisher.

1   2   3   4   5   6   7   8   9   10

ISBN 0-8251-6072-3

Copyright © 2006

J. Weston Walch, Publisher

P.O. Box 658 • Portland, Maine 04104-0658

www.walch.com

Printed in the United States of America

Table of Contents

iii

The **Daily Warm-Ups series** is a wonderful way to turn extra classroom minutes into valuable learning time. The 180 quick activities—one for each day of the school year—practice social studies skills. These daily activities may be used at the very beginning of class to get students into learning mode, near the end of class to make good educational use of that transitional time, in the middle of class to shift gears between lessons—or whenever else you have minutes that now go unused.

Daily Warm-Ups are easy-to-use reproducibles—simply photocopy the day's activity and distribute it. Or make a transparency of the activity and project it on the board. You may want to use the activities for extra-credit points or as a check on the social studies skills that are built and acquired over time.

However you choose to use them, *Daily Warm-Ups* are a convenient and useful supplement to your regular lesson plans. Make every minute of your class time count!

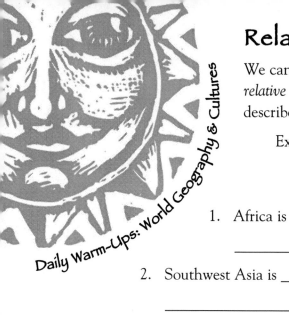

Relative Location

We can describe a place in relation to other places. This is called *relative location*. For each place named below, write a sentence that describes its location in relation to at least two other places.

Example: Europe is northeast of South America and southwest of Central Asia.

1. Africa is _____
   _____

2. Southwest Asia is _____
   _____

3. North America is _____
   _____

4. East Asia is _____
   _____

1

Distance and Scale

Look at the map of Belgium below. Choose three pairs of cities on the map. Then use the map scale to find the approximate distance between each pair of cities. Write your answers on the lines.

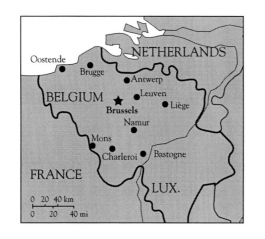

2

1. City 1: _____ City 2: _____ Distance: _____

2. City 1: _____ City 2: _____ Distance: _____

3. City 1: _____ City 2: _____ Distance: _____

Maps and Symbols

Look at the map below. Place-names have been added to the map, but the symbols that identify them have not yet been drawn on the map. Use the key to decide which symbol should be used for each place. Then draw the symbols at the appropriate places on the map.

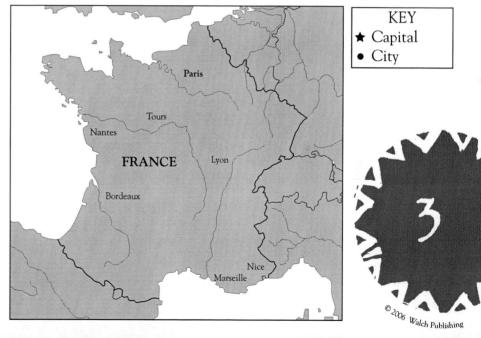

KEY
★ Capital
● City

Paris

Tours

Nantes

FRANCE

Lyon

Bordeaux

Nice

Marseille

3

Geography Terms

Each term below is used to describe one aspect of geography. Write **C** for climate, **M** for mapmaking, or **L** for landforms on the line before each term.

_____ 1. canyon

_____ 2. coordinates

_____ 3. plateau

_____ 4. projection

_____ 5. rainfall

_____ 6. scale

_____ 7. temperature

_____ 8. valley

_____ 9. wind patterns

4

Using Coordinates

Look at the map of Egypt below. Use the coordinates given to find the locations of these Egyptian cities. Place a dot at each city's location, and write the city's name beside the dot.

City	Latitude	Longitude
Alexandria	31° 13' N	29° 58' E
Cairo	30° 1' N	31° 14' E
Luxor	25° 41' N	32° 38' E
Port Said	31° 16' N	32° 18' E
Siwah	29° 11' N	25° 31' E

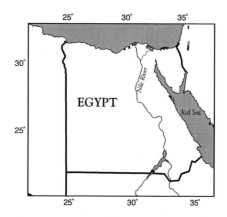

Absolute Location

Absolute location is the exact position on Earth where a place can be found. It is usually shown by using coordinates for latitude and longitude. No two places have the same absolute location.

Match each place named in the left column with its latitude and longitude in the right columns. Write the correct letter on the line.

	Place		Latitude	Longitude
___	1. Berlin, Germany	a.	35° 15' S	149° 8' E
___	2. Canberra, Australia	b.	52° 30' N	13° 25' E
___	3. Harare, Zimbabwe	c.	0° 15' S	78° 35' W
___	4. Quito, Ecuador	d.	35° 45' N	129° 45' E
___	5. Tokyo, Japan	e.	17° 43' S	31° 2' E

6

Daily Warm-Ups: World Geography & Cultures

Where Are You?

In geographic terms, location refers to a position on Earth's surface. What is the location of the place where you live? Draw a simple map of your state or province. On the map, mark the location of the city or town where you live.

7

Factors That Affect Population Growth

The table below gives some information about the population in three countries: Argentina, Poland, and Tanzania. In 2005, all three countries had about the same population size.

Study the table. Then use it to answer the questions that follow.

Country	Total Poulation (2005)	Age distribution			Fertility rate	Life expectancy at birth	Death rate
		0–14 yrs.	15–64 yrs.	65+ yrs.			
Argentina	39,537,943	25.6%	63.9%	10.6%	2.19	75.91	7.56
Poland	38,635,144	16.7%	70.3%	13.0%	1.39	74.74	10.01
Tanzania	36,766,356	44.0%	53.4%	2.6%	5.06	45.24	16.71

8

Assuming that all rates stay the same, will these three countries still have about the same population size in 2050? Why or why not?

World Population

How has the population of the world changed over the centuries? The table below gives estimated figures for the population of the world at different times in history. Use the figures to create a line graph that shows changes in world population.

Year	Population (in millions)
400	190
500	190
600	200
700	207
800	220
900	226
1000	254
1100	301
1200	360
1300	360
1400	350
1500	425
1600	545
1700	600
1800	813
1900	1550
2000	6060

9

© 2006 Walch Publishing

Push-Pull Factors

Push-pull factors are events and conditions that either force (push) people to move away from a place or strongly attract (pull) them to move to a new location.

Think of one period in the last century when large numbers of people moved from one place to another. What push and pull factors were operating to cause this migration?

Period: _____

Push factors: _____

_____

_____

_____

Pull factors: _____

_____

_____

_____

10

People and Environment

People have found ways to live in all sorts of environments, from hot to cold, from wet to dry. Over the years, people adapt to their environments. But people also adapt their environments to fit their needs.

Think of all the ways that humans change their environment. List as many of them as you can.

11

Nonrenewable Energy Sources

Humans have found many ways to generate energy. Some of these energy sources are nonrenewable. Once they have been used, they cannot be replaced.

Name three nonrenewable energy sources and some of the things they are used to power.

_____

_____

_____

_____

Can you suggest any ways to conserve these nonrenewable resources?

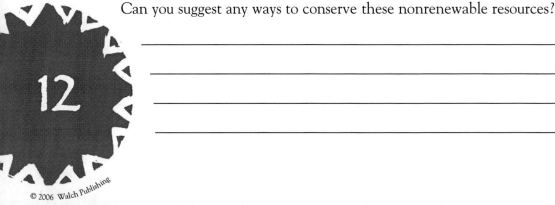

12

_____

_____

_____

_____

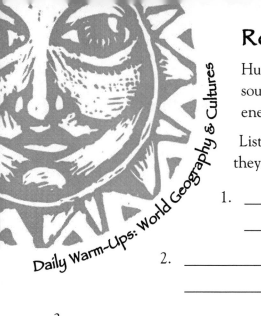

Renewable Energy Sources

Humans have found many ways to generate energy. Some energy sources are renewable. If used carefully, the source can produce energy more than once.

List three renewable energy sources below and some of the things they are used to power.

1. _____

   _____

2. _____

   _____

3. _____

   _____

13

Pandemic

At first, the flu epidemic didn't seem unusual; a few people die from the flu most years. But doctors in 1918 noticed something disturbing. Usually, the flu hits people with weak immune systems, such as children or the elderly. The 1918 flu struck mostly young, healthy people. Hundreds were sick, then thousands, then millions. Rather than an epidemic, this was a *pandemic*—a worldwide epidemic. Doctors were helpless against the disease.

Health authorities tried to stop the spread of the disease. In the United States, stores could not hold sales, which drew crowds. People wore gauze masks in public. Nurses, doctors, and hospital rooms were in short supply; so were coffins and gravediggers. In just over a year, the flu killed about 40 million people worldwide—more than any other single event in world history.

Then, in spring 1919, the disease stopped suddenly. The pandemic was over.

Do you think a pandemic like the 1918 flu pandemic could happen again? Why or why not? Write two or three sentences explaining your answer.

14

World Languages

From earliest times, people have felt the need to communicate. Different areas developed different languages. Some developed into whole families of related languages. Some language families include dozens of related languages.

Match each language family in the box with its description below. Write the correct letter on the line.

Language Families	
a. Sino-Tibetan	c. Malayo-Polynesian
b. Indo-European	d. Niger-Congo

____ 1. This language family has members across Europe and South Asia. Languages in this family include English, Spanish, Greek, and Hindi.

____ 2. This family includes African languages south of the Sahara, such as Swahili, Shona, Xhosa, and Zulu.

____ 3. This important Asian language family includes the language with the most speakers in the world, Mandarin.

____ 4. This family of over 1,000 languages is found in East Asia and across the Indian and Pacific oceans. It includes Indonesian and Hawaiian.

15

World Geography: True or False?

Decide if each statement below is true (**T**) or false (**F**). Write the appropriate letter on the line before each statement. Rewrite any false statements to make them true.

____ 1.   The study of geography only involves knowing about location—where places are on a map.

____ 2.   Culture includes things such as housing, sports, and language.

____ 3.   In geography, the word *customs* always refers to a border check when you enter a country.

____ 4.   Patterns of emigration and immigration are part of the geographic theme of movement.

____ 5.   Maps use many imaginary lines to help make sense of the world.

16

The Water Cycle

Water is one of Earth's most precious resources. Without it, life as humans know it would not exist. Earth's water is constantly cycling through the atmosphere.

The diagram below shows a simplified version of the water cycle. Label the four major stages that water goes through in this cycle.

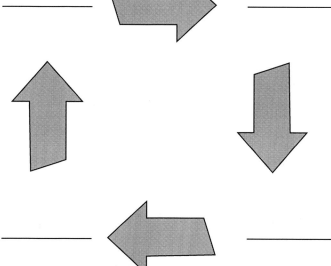

17

Where Would You See . . . ?

Plants need certain conditions in which to grow. Certain plants favor each climate type listed below. List as many of each as you can. The first one has been started for you.

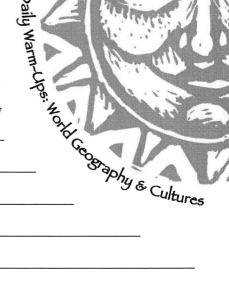

Climate Type	Plants
1. tropical rain forest	tall hardwood trees such as mahogany and teak; _____
2. savanna	_____
3. marine west coast	_____
4. Mediterranean	_____
5. moist continental	_____
6. tundra	_____
7. desert	_____
8. taiga	_____
9. steppe	_____

18

Daily Warm-Ups: World Geography & Cultures

Climate and Weather

Each phrase below is the definition for a term used to describe climate or weather. For each one, identify the term that is being defined. Write the term on the line before the definition.

_____ 1. the transition zone between two air masses of different density or temperature

_____ 2. a violently rotating column of air, often in the form of a funnel cloud, with wind speeds of up to 300 miles per hour

_____ 3. a period of abnormally dry weather

_____ 4. any form of water, such as rain, snow, sleet, or hail, that falls to Earth's surface

_____ 5. the long-term weather pattern of a place or region, including temperature, rainfall, and wind

19

Climate Zones

Match each climate zone with its description below. Write the correct letter on the line provided.

	Climate Zone		Description
___ 1.	arid	a.	hot all year, 50–100 inches annual rainfall
___ 2.	semiarid	b.	hot summers, cool winters, 23 inches annual rainfall
___ 3.	tropical	c.	hot days, cold nights, 5 inches annual rainfall
___ 4.	Mediterranean	d.	cool summers, very cold winters, 17 inches annual rainfall
___ 5.	tundra	e.	hot summers, cool winters, 50 inches annual rainfall
___ 6.	humid subtropical	f.	hot summers, mild to cold winters, 18 inches annual rainfall
___ 7.	subarctic	g.	cold summers, very cold winters, 16 inches annual rainfall

20

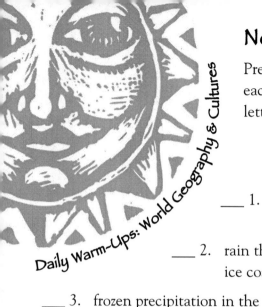

Not Rain, nor Snow, nor Sleet . . .

Precipitation can take many forms, both liquid and frozen. Match each term in the box with its description below. Write the correct letter on the line.

a. drizzle	b. freezing rain	c. graupel (snow pellets)
d. hail	e. rain	f. sleet g. snow

___ 1. precipitation in liquid water drops, usually more than 0.5 mm in diameter

___ 2. rain that falls in liquid form but freezes on the ground to form an ice coating

___ 3. frozen precipitation in the form of six-sided white or translucent ice crystals

___ 4. frozen precipitation in the form of balls or irregular lumps of ice, with a diameter of 5 mm or more

___ 5. precipitation consisting of round, white, opaque ice particles

___ 6. very small, numerous, uniformly distributed water drops that may appear to float while following air currents

___ 7. precipitation in the form of a mixture of rain and snow

21

What's the Question?

Each statement below is the answer to a question about geography. For each one, write the original question.

1. an imaginary line that divides the globe into Southern and Northern hemispheres

   _____

2. one of the four points of the compass: north, south, east, and west

   _____

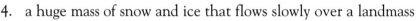

3. subarctic coniferous forests found just south of the tundra

   _____

4. a huge mass of snow and ice that flows slowly over a landmass

   _____

5. a rocklike marine ridge or mound in warm seas made primarily from skeletal fragments of marine organisms, built up and compacted over a long period

   _____

22

North America Map

The map below shows part of North America, but no place-names have been written on the map. Use your knowledge of the area to label the countries, capital cities, and three major bodies of water.

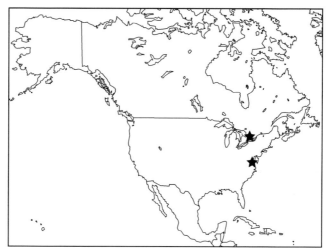

23

Absolute Location

Absolute location is the exact position on Earth where a place can be found. It is usually shown by using coordinates for latitude and longitude. No two places have the same absolute location.

Match each place named in the left column with its latitude and longitude in the right columns. Write the correct letter on the line.

24

Place		Latitude	Longitude
___ 1. Calgary, Canada	a.	52° 55' N	66° 52' W
___ 2. Cincinnati, Ohio	b.	39° 6' N	84° 31' W
___ 3. Dallas, Texas	c.	51° 0' N	114° 10' W
___ 4. San Diego, California	d.	32° 47' N	96° 49' W
___ 5. Wabush, Canada	e.	32° 43' N	117° 9' W

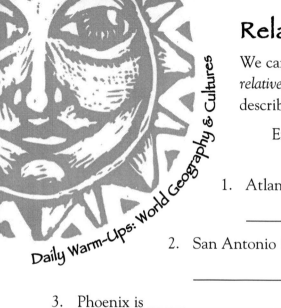

Daily Warm-Ups: World Geography & Cultures

Relative Location

We can describe a place in relation to other places. This is called *relative location*. For each place named below, write a sentence that describes its location in relation to at least two other places.

Example: St. Louis is southwest of Indianapolis and northeast of Dallas.

1. Atlanta is _____

    _____

2. San Antonio is _____

    _____

3. Phoenix is _____

    _____

4. San Francisco is _____

    _____

25

Landforms

The map below shows some of the physical features of the western United States. They include four mountain ranges, three deserts, one river, and one lake. Label each one.

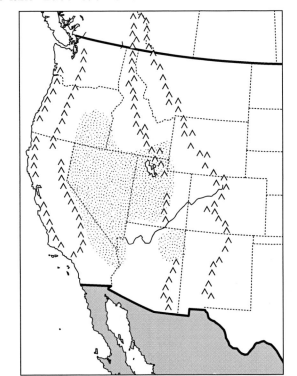

26

Northeastern States and Capitals

Some states of the Northeast and their capitals are listed below. Write the letter of the correct capital city on the line before each state.

State		Capital City	
___ 1.	Connecticut	a.	Albany
___ 2.	Maine	b.	Augusta
___ 3.	Massachusetts	c.	Boston
___ 4.	New Hampshire	d.	Concord
___ 5.	New Jersey	e.	Harrisburg
___ 6.	New York	f.	Hartford
___ 7.	Pennsylvania	g.	Montpelier
___ 8.	Rhode Island	h.	Providence
___ 9.	Vermont	i.	Trenton

27

The U.S. Census

A *census* is an investigation or count of a population. In the United States, censuses have been taken regularly since 1790. Today, the U.S. Census Bureau takes a complete census of the U.S. population every ten years. Information provided by the census includes the number of people who live in an area; their distribution by age, race, and sex; and economic indicators.

Almost 12,000 people work full-time for the Census Bureau. Every ten years, when the census is taken, the workforce expands. In 2000, about 860,000 temporary workers were hired.

Why do you think the government considers knowing about population so important? List as many reasons as you can think of.

28

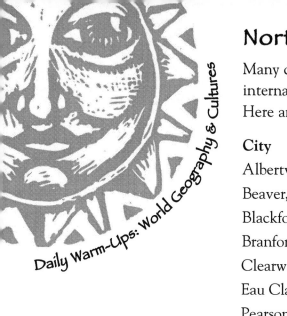

North American Nicknames

Many cities have nicknames that lay claim to being the international capital of something, such as an industry or a hobby. Here are some U.S. cities that make this kind of claim:

City	Nickname
Albertville, AL	Fire hydrant capital of the world
Beaver, OK	Cow chip throwing capital of the world
Blackfoot, ID	Potato capital of the world
Branford, FL	Cave diving capital of the world
Clearwater, FL	Lightning capital of the world
Eau Claire, MI	Cherry pit spitting capital of the world
Pearsonville, CA	Hubcap capital of the world

Think of a city that you are familiar with. Give it a nickname claiming it is the international capital of something. Then explain why it deserves this title.

The city _____ deserves the title _____

capital of the world because _____

_____

29

Growth of the Suburbs

At the beginning of the twentieth century, most Americans lived in rural areas. Over the next few decades, this started to change. By about 1920, half the population lived and worked in cities. Half lived in rural areas and worked on farms.

During the 1920s and 1930s, a new place to live developed: the *suburb*, an area on the edge of a city. Suburbs are neither urban nor rural. Most have many houses, each with a separate yard. People live in suburbs, but usually commute to another area to work.

In 1950, less than a quarter of the U.S. population lived in suburban areas. Almost a third lived in rural areas. By 1990, only one fifth lived in rural areas. Half of U.S. residents lived in the suburbs.

Several factors contributed to this change. Name as many of them as you can.

Extreme Commuters

In the United States, most workers live and work in the same area. In heavy traffic areas, it may take them a long time to get to work, but the distance they travel isn't very great. However, a growing number of workers travel more than 100 miles to work. They often live in one state and work in another, spending several hours each day going to and from work.

What reasons do you think would motivate a person to live in a place so far from work? List as many reasons as you can.

31

City Slogans

More and more, cities are using slogans to market their appeal as places to visit. A successful slogan expresses something about a city's character or personality. Slogans are unique and original in some way, and inspire people to visit the city, live there, or learn more about it. For example, the slogan of Hershey, Pennsylvania, is "The sweetest place on Earth." The slogan of Happy, Texas, is "The town without a frown."

Create a slogan or motto for one of the cities listed below. Your slogan should be specific, unique, and compelling.

Augusta, Maine

Columbus, Ohio

Salt Lake City, Utah

Toronto, Ontario

Vancouver, British Columbia

32

City: _____

Slogan: _____

Most and Least Affordable Areas

The cost of living varies from region to region across the United States. Cost of living includes many different factors, including the cost of housing.

The table below shows the ten most affordable and least affordable U.S. metropolitan areas with fewer than 500,000 residents. (Some of these areas include more than one city or town.) Look at the table. Why do you think some of these areas are more affordable than others? Write one or two sentences for your answer.

10 Most Affordable Metro Areas	10 Least Affordable Metro Areas
1. Davenport-Moline-Rock Island, IA-IL	1. Merced, CA
2. Cumberland, MD	2. Modesto, CA
3. Lima, OH	3. Salinas, CA
4. Mansfield, OH	4. Santa Barbara-Santa Maria, CA
5. Lansing-East Lansing, MI	5. Santa Cruz-Watsonville, CA
6. Canton-Massillon, OH	6. Yuba City, CA
7. Saginaw-Saginaw Township North, MI	7. San Luis Obispo-Paso Robles, CA
8. Flint, MI	8. Santa Rosa-Petaluma, CA
9. Duluth, MN	9. Vallejo-Fairfield, CA
10. Champaign-Urbana, IL	10. Barnstable, MA

33

True or False?

Decide if each statement below is true (**T**) or false (**F**). Write the appropriate letter on the line before each statement. Rewrite any false statements to make them true.

___ 1. There are more different climate zones in the United States than in any other country.

___ 2. The northernmost point in the continental United States is in Maine.

___ 3. The United States and Canada are so heavily industrialized that there is no longer any land for farming.

___ 4. A band of steep mountains runs from north to south through Canada and the United States.

___ 5. Most people in both the United States and Canada live in urban areas.

34

What's Your Region?

A *region* is an area with one or more common features or characteristics. They may be physical characteristics, such as climate or soil type. They may be cultural characteristics, such as language or economy.

In what region do you live? _____

What are the boundaries of this region? _____

_____

What features or characteristics define this region? _____

_____

_____

_____

35

Emergency!

In California, people need to be prepared for earthquakes and mudslides. In Florida, they watch for hurricanes. Other areas face the threat of blizzards, flash floods, and wildfires. No matter where people live, there is a risk of some kind of natural disaster. In extreme cases, people may need to evacuate, or leave the area.

What types of natural hazards does your area face? _____

_____

If you had to evacuate your home, where would you go? How would you get there? What would you take with you? Write a plan for what you (and your family) would do if a natural disaster struck your area.

36

Daily Warm-Ups: World Geography & Cultures

Changes in the Environment

For thousands of years, people have adapted their environments to fit their needs. This can include cutting down trees; plowing fields; moving rocks; erecting buildings; building roads, bridges, and tunnels; and more.

Choose a place in Canada or the United States where people have modified their environment. List all the ways in which the environment has been changed to meet the needs of the people who live there.

Place: _____

Changes: _____

_____

_____

_____

_____

_____

_____

37

Name That Region

The map below shows a region of the United States that is known for a certain weather phenomenon. In fact, the region has a nickname based on this kind of weather. What is the nickname for this region?

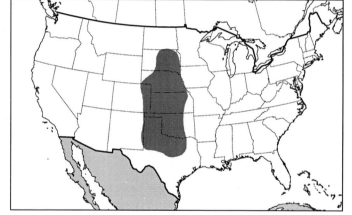

38

What's the Question?

Each statement below is the answer to a question about U.S. geography. For each one, give the original question.

1. a continuous urban area, where one city merges into the next, such as the region between Boston, Massachusetts, and Washington, D.C.

    _____

2. a government project begun in 1933, with the aim of controlling floods and using water to provide electricity, that now provides power to nearly 8.5 million people

    _____

3. the only one of the five Great Lakes that is completely within the United States, not Canada

    _____

4. the process by which a country's population changes from rural to urban as people move from the country to the city

    _____

5. the northernmost state in the United States, separated from the rest of the country by western Canada

    _____

39

What's the Question?

Each statement below is the answer to a question about the geography of Canada. For each one, write the original question.

1. a 2,342-mile-long system of canals, dams, and locks on the St. Lawrence River, opened in 1959, that allows oceangoing vessels to pass from the Atlantic Ocean to the Great Lakes

   _____

2. the west coast city that is home to more than one quarter of Canada's Chinese-Canadian community

   _____

3. Canada's newest province, created in 1999, home to many of Canada's Inuit residents

   _____

40

4. the area off the coasts of Newfoundland and Nova Scotia that is among the world's richest fishing areas

   _____

5. Canada's largest province in terms of area, home to much of the country's French-Canadian population

   _____

Latin America Map

The map below shows part of northwestern Latin America, but no place-names have been written on the map. Use your knowledge of the area to write each name where it belongs.

Countries	Cities
COLOMBIA	Bogotá
ECUADOR	Caracas
GUYANA	Georgetown
PERU	Lima
VENEZUELA	Quito

41

Absolute Location

Absolute location is the exact position on Earth where a place can be found. It is usually shown by using coordinates for latitude and longitude. No two places have the same absolute location.

Match each place named in the left column with its latitude and longitude in the right columns. Write the correct letter on the line.

	Place		Latitude	Longitude
___ 1.	Arequipa, Peru	a.	34° 50' S	56° 11' W
___ 2.	Brasília, Brazil	b.	15° 47' S	47° 55' W
___ 3.	Cali, Colombia	c.	19° 3' N	98° 12' W
___ 4.	Montevideo, Uruguay	d.	3° 25' N	76° 35' W
___ 5.	Puebla, Mexico	e.	16° 20' S	71° 30' W

42

Relative Location

We can describe a place in relation to other places. This is called *relative location*. For each place named below, write a sentence that describes its location in relation to at least two other places.

Example: Sucre is southwest of Brasília and southeast of La Paz.

1. Buenos Aires is _____

   _____

2. Lima is _____

   _____

3. Bogotá is _____

   _____

4. Quito is _____

   _____

43

Landforms

The map below shows some of the physical features of Mexico. These include two important peninsulas, three rivers, three major bodies of water, and three mountain ranges. Label each one.

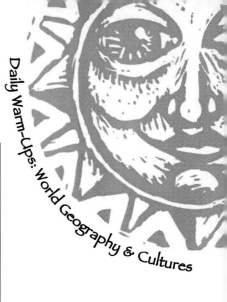

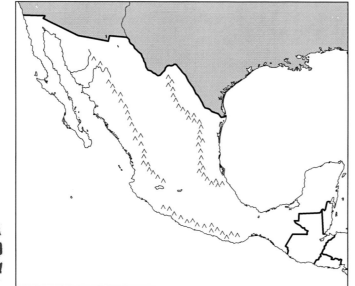

Geography Terms

Each definition below describes a word used to discuss the geography of Latin America. Write the term that fits each definition on the line.

_____ 1. a series of highland valleys and plateaus in the Andes of Peru and Bolivia

_____ 2. a group of mountain ranges that run side by side

_____ 3. an open, grassy plain

_____ 4. grasslands region in Argentina and Uruguay

_____ 5. a range of mountains

45

Countries and Capitals

Some Latin American countries and their capitals are listed below. Write the letter of the correct capital city on the line before each country.

	Country		Capital City
_____	1. Argentina	a.	Asunción
_____	2. Brazil	b.	Bogotá
_____	3. Chile	c.	Brasília
_____	4. Colombia	d.	Buenos Aires
_____	5. Ecuador	e.	Caracas
_____	6. El Salvador	f.	Lima
_____	7. Nicaragua	g.	Managua
_____	8. Paraguay	h.	Quito
_____	9. Peru	i.	Santiago
_____	10. Venezuela	j.	San Salvador

46

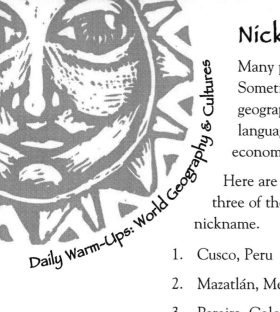

Nicknames

Many places have nicknames in addition to their actual names. Sometimes these nicknames refer to some aspect of physical geography. Sometimes they refer to human characteristics, such as language, architecture, or music. Sometimes they refer to the economic activity of the city.

Here are some Latin American cities and their nicknames. Choose three of the cities. For each one, explain the origin of the city's nickname.

1.	Cusco, Peru	The Imperial City
2.	Mazatlán, Mexico	The Pearl of the Pacific
3.	Pereira, Colombia	Pearl of the Otun
4.	Quebradillas, Puerto Rico	The Pirate's Hideout
5.	São Paulo, Brazil	Brazil's Locomotive
6.	Taxco, Mexico	The Silver Capital of the World
7.	Ushuaia, Argentina	The End of the World

47

Changes in the Environment

For thousands of years, people have adapted their environments to fit their needs. This can include cutting down trees; plowing fields; moving rocks; erecting buildings; building roads, bridges, and tunnels; and more.

Choose a place in Latin America where people have modified their environment. List all the ways in which the environment has been changed to meet the needs of the people who live there.

Place: _____

Changes: _____

_____

_____

_____

_____

_____

48

Regions

Latin America is a general term used to describe a large geographic area. Within this large area, many different regions can be identified. However, based on physical geography, Latin America can be divided into three major regions. Name these regions. For each one, name at least three countries within the region.

Region 1: _____

    Country 1: _____

    Country 2: _____

    Country 3: _____

Region 2: _____

    Country 1: _____

    Country 2: _____

    Country 3: _____

Region 3: _____

    Country 1: _____

    Country 2: _____

    Country 3: _____

49

Population of Argentina

The table below shows how Argentina's population has changed in different decades. The figure for 2010 is an estimate.

Use the figures to create a line graph that shows changes in the population of Argentina. Then answer the question that follows.

Year	Population (in millions)
1900	4,542
1910	6,615
1920	8,861
1930	11,896
1940	14,401
1950	17,150
1960	20,759
1970	23,364
1980	27,949
1990	32,547
2000	36,955
2010 (est)	38,896

50

Based on your graph, what do you think the population of Argentina will be in 2020? _____

Independence

For years, most of Latin America was ruled by countries in Europe. Then, in the early 1800s, a wave of revolutions swept the region. One after another, the colonies became independent.

The countries listed below all gained their independence during the 1800s. Use the information to create a time line. Give your time line a descriptive title.

1816	Argentina
1825	Bolivia
1822	Brazil
1818	Chile
1819	Colombia
1830	Ecuador
1821	Mexico
1811	Paraguay
1821	Peru
1828	Uruguay
1830	Venezuela

51

© 2006 Walch Publishing

Words from the Maya

When the Spanish first arrived in Mexico and Central America, hundreds of languages were spoken in the region. The conquerors introduced their own language, Spanish. However, they also took some words from the Maya. Versions of some of these words have since passed into English.

Here are some words that have been adopted from the Maya. They are all names for things that were found only in the Americas, not in Europe. Can you identify the English word that came from each Mayan word? Write it on the line before the Mayan word.

_____ 1. auakatl (a food)

_____ 2. chokolatl (a food)

_____ 3. koyotl (an animal)

_____ 4. tomatl (a food)

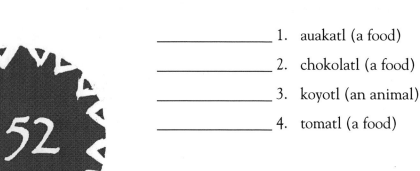

52

Everyday Spanish

Spanish is spoken in many parts of Latin America. Some common Spanish phrases are given below in the left column. Match each one with its English translation in the right column. Write the correct letter on the line.

___ 1. Buenos días.

___ 2. ¿Cómo se llamo usted?

___ 3. Mucho gusto.

___ 4. ¿Cómo está usted?

___ 5. Muy bien, gracias.

___ 6. Adíos.

a. Very well, thanks.

b. Good-bye.

c. How are you?

d. What is your name?

e. Nice to meet you.

f. Hello.

53

Proverbs

Different cultures often use proverbs to express the same ideas. Here are some proverbs from Mexico. For each one, think of another proverb that expresses the same idea. Write it on the lines under the Mexican proverb.

1. Quien pide no escoge. (The person who pleads does not choose.) _____

   _____

2. Hombre prevenido vale por dos. (A man warned in advance is worth two.)

   _____

   _____

54

3. Quien bien va, no tuerce. (If it's going well, don't change it.)

   _____

   _____

True or False?

Decide if each statement below is true (**T**) or false (**F**). Write the appropriate letter on the line before each statement. Rewrite any false statements to make them true.

___ 1. The longest river in the Western Hemisphere, the Amazon, carries more water than any other river.

___ 2. The countries of Latin America all have similar climates, landforms, and resources.

___ 3. The Andes Mountains, which run along the west coast of South America, affect the climate of countries in the region.

___ 4. Nearly a quarter of the world's animal species live in South America.

___ 5. Spanish is the primary language of Brazil.

55

What's the Question?

Each statement below is the answer to a question about the geography of Latin America. For each one, write the original question on the line.

1. the longest mountain chain in the world

   _____

2. the 3,900-mile-long river that collects water from almost forty percent of South America's landmass before it empties into the Atlantic Ocean

   _____

3. flat, fertile plains that cover 300,000 square miles between the Atlantic Ocean and the Andes Mountains

   _____

4. the narrow body of water that separates South America from Tierra del Fuego, named for the Portuguese explorer who sailed through it in 1520

   _____

56

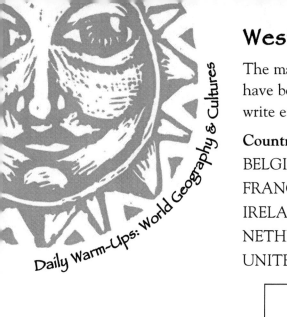

Western Europe Map

The map below shows part of Western Europe, but no place-names have been written on the map. Use your knowledge of the area to write each name where it belongs.

Countries

BELGIUM

FRANCE

IRELAND

NETHERLANDS

UNITED KINGDOM

Cities

Amsterdam

Brussels

Dublin

London

Paris

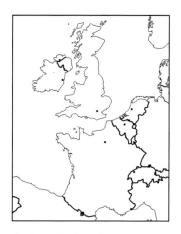

57

Absolute Location

Absolute location is the exact position on Earth where a place can be found. It is usually shown by using coordinates for latitude and longitude. No two places have the same absolute location.

Match each place named in the left column with its latitude and longitude in the right columns. Write the correct letter on the line.

	Place		Latitude	Longitude
___ 1.	Carcassonne, France	a.	64° 10' N	21° 57' W
___ 2.	Copenhagen, Denmark	b.	43° 13' N	2° 20' E
___ 3.	Reykjavik, Iceland	c.	45° 3' N	7° 40' E
___ 4.	Tralee, Ireland	d.	55° 41' N	12° 34' E
___ 5.	Turin, Italy	e.	52° 16' N	9° 42' W

58

Relative Location

We can describe a place in relation to other places. This is called *relative location*. For each place named below, write a sentence that describes its location in relation to at least two other places.

Example: Paris is southwest of Copenhagen and southeast of London.

1. Berlin is _____

   _____

2. Lisbon is _____

   _____

3. Rome is _____

   _____

4. Dublin is _____

   _____

59

Landforms

The map below shows some of the physical features of Italy. They include two major mountain ranges, two major rivers, and four seas. Label each one.

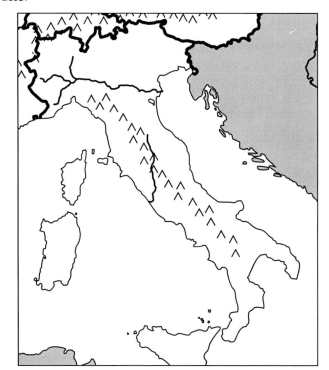

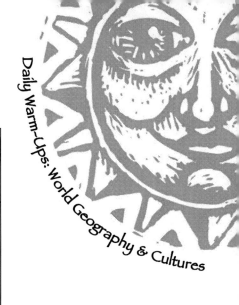

60

Regions

Regions are places that share at least one common characteristic. They may share a physical characteristic, such as soil type or landforms. They may share a cultural characteristic, such as religion, language, or economy.

There are many different regions in Western Europe. List as many of them as you can in the space below. Include both physical and cultural regions.

61

Countries and Capitals

Some Western European countries and their capitals are listed below. Write the letter of the correct capital city on the line before each country.

	Country		Capital City
____ 1.	Belgium	a.	Athens
____ 2.	Denmark	b.	Berlin
____ 3.	France	c.	Brussels
____ 4.	Germany	d.	Copenhagen
____ 5.	Greece	e.	Lisbon
____ 6.	Iceland	f.	Madrid
____ 7.	Italy	g.	Paris
____ 8.	Portugal	h.	Reykjavik
____ 9.	Spain	i.	Rome
____ 10.	Sweden	j.	Stockholm

62

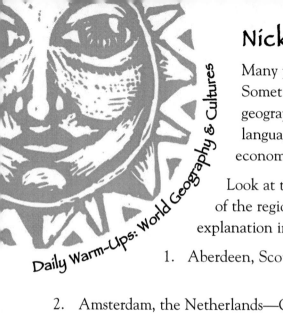

Nicknames

Many places have nicknames in addition to their actual names. Sometimes these nicknames refer to some aspect of physical geography. Sometimes they refer to human characteristics, such as language, architecture, or music. Sometimes they refer to the economic activity of the city.

Look at the nicknames for places listed below. Use your knowledge of the region to decide how each city got its nickname. Write your explanation in the space below.

1. Aberdeen, Scotland—The Oil Capital of Europe

2. Amsterdam, the Netherlands—Gateway to Europe

3. The Hague, the Netherlands—City of Peace and Justice

4. Milan, Italy—The Fashion Capital of the World

5. Rome, Italy—The City of the Seven Hills

63

Oranges and Lemons

An old English nursery rhyme refers to the bells that rang in certain London neighborhoods. Read the rhyme. Then write the letter of the bell next to its neighborhood below.

> a. Oranges and lemons/Say the bells of St. Clements
> b. You owe me five farthings/ Say the bells of St. Martins
> c. When will you pay me?/ Say the bells of Old Bailey
> d. When I grow rich/ Say the bells of Shoreditch
> e. When will that be?/ Say the bells of Stepney
> f. I'm sure I don't know/Says the great bell at Bow

_____ 1. Cannon Street was famous for moneylenders.

_____ 2. Cheapside: In the heart of old London, a nightly curfew once rang on the bells of St. Mary-le-Bow Church.

_____ 3. Eastcheap: Citrus fruit were once unloaded at the wharf here.

_____ 4. Hackney: The area near St. Leonard's Church was very poor.

_____ 5. Newgate: People who could not pay debts were tried on Bailey Street and imprisoned in Newgate Prison.

_____ 6. Stepney: Sailors and their families lived near St. Dunstan's.

64

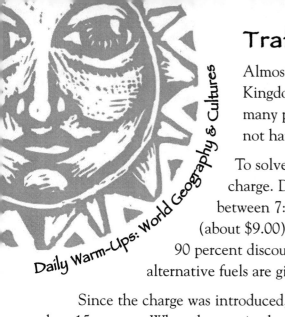

Traffic Management

Almost 7,500,000 people live in London, the capital of the United Kingdom. By 2003, traffic in London was unmanageable. Too many people were driving into the city every day. The roads could not handle the traffic.

To solve the problem, London's mayor introduced a congestion charge. Drivers of private cars who want to go into the city center between 7:00 A.M. and 6:30 P.M. on a weekday must pay a fee of £5 (about $9.00). People who live in the congestion zone are given a 90 percent discount on the fee. Scooters, bicycles, and cars that run on alternative fuels are given a 100 percent discount.

Since the charge was introduced, traffic in central London has decreased by more than 15 percent. What changes in the way people commute might account for this decrease? Write your answers below.

65

Languages

Most languages in Western Europe are members of the Indo-European language family. Over the centuries, three major language divisions developed in the region: Romance, Germanic, and Celtic languages. Romance languages developed from Latin, the ancient language of Rome. Germanic languages are offshoots of a language that developed in southern Scandinavia. Celtic languages are descended from Proto-Celtic or Common Celtic, which was once spoken across much of Europe. Most European languages belong to one of these language divisions, but a few do not.

Some European languages are listed below. Decide if each one is a Romance language (**R**), a Germanic language (**G**), a Celtic language (**C**), or is unrelated (**U**). Write the letter of the language division on the line before each language.

66

___ 1. Basque	___ 7. Finnish	___ 13. Norwegian
___ 2. Breton	___ 8. French	___ 14. Portuguese
___ 3. Catalan	___ 9. German	___ 15. Scots-Gaelic
___ 4. Danish	___ 10. Icelandic	___ 16. Spanish
___ 5. Dutch	___ 11. Irish	___ 17. Swedish
___ 6. English	___ 12. Italian	___ 18. Welsh

Language Fragmentation

Most European languages are related to one another. They all developed from the same ancient parent language. But today, most of these languages are very different from one another. People who speak different languages cannot understand one another.

Think about the physical geography of Europe. How might it have affected the development of different languages? Write two or three sentences for your answer.

67

Changes in the Environment

For thousands of years, people have adapted their environments to fit their needs. This can include cutting down trees; plowing fields; moving rocks; erecting buildings; building roads, bridges, and tunnels; and more.

Choose a place in Western Europe where people have modified their environment. List all the ways the environment has been changed to meet the needs of the people who live there.

Place: _____

Changes: _____

_____

_____

_____

_____

_____

_____

68

Population of France

How has the population of France changed over the last century? The table below gives figures for France's population in different decades. The figure for 2010 is an estimate.

Use the figures to create a line graph that shows changes in the population of France. Then answer the question that follows.

Year	Population (in millions)
1900	38,900
1910	39,540
1920	39,000
1930	41,610
1940	39,000
1950	41,829
1960	45,684
1970	50,772
1980	53,880
1990	56,718
2000	59,330
2010 (est)	62,121

France's population dropped between 1910 and 1920, and again between 1930 and 1940. What do you think caused these drops?

69

Keeping Warm in Iceland

The climate of Iceland is cold, with long, dark winters. Most homes in Iceland are comfortably warm in winter. However, few of them use coal, oil, wood, or electricity for heat.

The graph below shows the breakdown of homes heated using different methods. One heat method is not labeled. Based on what you know about the geography of Iceland, what is this heat method? Write the name on the line in the graph.

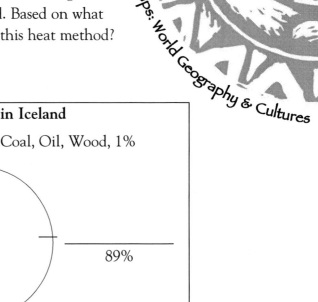

Home Heat in Iceland

Electricity, 10%

Coal, Oil, Wood, 1%

89%

70

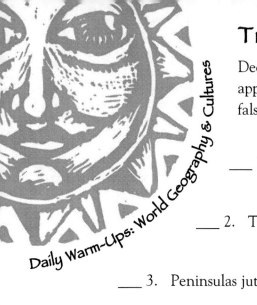

Daily Warm-Ups: World Geography & Cultures

True or False?

Decide if each statement below is true (**T**) or false (**F**). Write the appropriate letter on the line before each statement. Rewrite any false statements to make them true.

___ 1. The Pyrenees divide Italy from the rest of Europe.

___ 2. The fjords of Scandinavia were carved out by glaciers.

___ 3. Peninsulas jut out to the north, south, and west of Europe.

___ 4. There are no active volcanoes in Europe today.

___ 5. Spain's geography is dominated by its hot, dry central plateau.

71

What's the Question?

Each statement below is the answer to a question about the geography of Europe. For each one, write the original question.

1. the mountain range that separates Italy from the rest of mainland Europe

   _____

2. a tiny nation, just 180 square miles in area, in the Pyrenees Mountains between France and Spain

   _____

3. a 32-mile-long rail tunnel that runs under the English Channel

   _____

4. deep, steep-walled, sea inlets that characterize the coast of Norway

   _____

5. an arm of the Atlantic Ocean, located between Scotland, Norway, and Denmark in the north, that is an important source of oil

   _____

72

Eastern Europe Map

The map below shows part of Eastern Europe, but no place names have been written on the map. Use your knowledge of the area to write each name where it belongs.

Countries	Cities
CZECH REPUBLIC	Bratislava
HUNGARY	Budapest
POLAND	Ljubljana
SLOVAKIA	Prague
SLOVENIA	Warsaw

Absolute Location

Absolute location is the exact position on Earth where a place can be found. It is usually shown by using coordinates for latitude and longitude. No two places have the same absolute location.

Match each place named in the left column with its latitude and longitude in the right columns. Write the correct letter on the line.

	Place	Latitude	Longitude
___ 1.	Belgrade, Serbia and Montenegro	a. 44° 27' N	26° 10' E
___ 2.	Budapest, Hungary	b. 52° 13' N	21° 0' E
___ 3.	Bucharest, Romania	c. 42° 45' N	23° 20' E
___ 4.	Sofia, Bulgaria	d. 47° 29' N	19° 5' E
___ 5.	Warsaw, Poland	e. 44° 50' N	20° 37' E

74

Relative Location

We can describe a place in relation to other places. This is called *relative location*. For each place named below, write a sentence that describes its location in relation to at least two other places.

Example: Warsaw is northeast of Prague and northwest of Bucharest.

1. Sofia is _____

_____

2. Tirane is _____

_____

3. Budapest is _____

_____

4. Zagreb is _____

_____

75

Landforms

The map below shows some of the physical features of Poland. They include two important rivers, two mountain ranges, and one sea. Label each one.

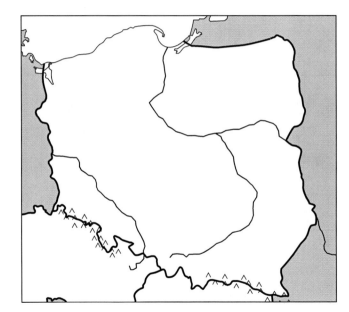

76

Fill in the Blanks

Choose the correct name from the box to complete each statement below.

Balkan	Danube	Transylvania	Vistula	Yugoslavia

1. The _____ River rises in Poland's Carpathian Mountains and flows more than 680 miles before emptying into the Baltic Sea.

2. The most famous river of Eastern Europe is the 1,766-mile-long _____ , which flows through Austria, Bulgaria, Croatia, Germany, Hungary, Romania, Serbia and Montenegro, Slovakia, and Slovenia before emptying into the Black Sea.

3. The _____ and Rhodope Mountains span most of Bulgaria.

4. During the 1990s, the country of _____ broke apart into five separate countries: Slovenia, Croatia, Macedonia, Bosnia and Herzegovina, and Serbia and Montenegro.

5. The region of _____ in Romania is the source of many stories, but the name means simply "across the forest."

77

A Changing Economy

Until the early 1990s, most countries of Eastern Europe had communist governments. These governments controlled the economy, as well as most other aspects of society. The fall of communism brought new freedom to many Eastern Europeans. But it also brought new problems.

What problems do you think this change brought to Eastern Europe? List as many as you can think of.

78

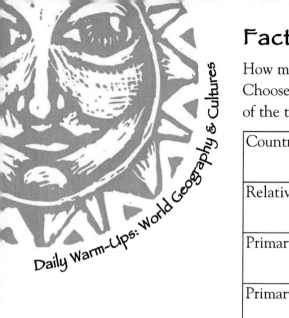

Facts About Eastern Europe

How much do you know about the countries of Eastern Europe? Choose one Eastern European country. Write its name at the top of the table below. Then fill in as much information as you can.

Country's name	
Relative location	
Primary language	
Primary religion	
Government	
Main industry	
Currency	

79

Physical Features

Each statement below describes a physical feature found in Eastern Europe. Write the name of the feature on the line.

1. This branch of the Alps runs from north to south along the Adriatic coast from Slovenia to Albania.

    _____

2. The mountain range that runs from west to east across Romania is the fictional home of a famous count. _____

3. This river rises in Germany and flows across many countries of Eastern Europe before emptying into the Black Sea. _____

4. The borders of many countries on this peninsula between the Black Sea and the Adriatic Sea have been redrawn several times in the last century.

    _____

5. This huge plain stretches from France in the west to Russia in the east.

    _____

80

Countries and Capitals

Some Eastern European countries and their capitals are listed below. Write the letter of the correct capital city on the line before each country.

	Country		Capital City
_____	1. Albania	a.	Bratislava
_____	2. Bulgaria	b.	Bucharest
_____	3. Croatia	c.	Budapest
_____	4. Czech Republic	d.	Ljubljana
_____	5. Hungary	e.	Prague
_____	6. Macedonia	f.	Skopje
_____	7. Poland	g.	Sofia
_____	8. Romania	h.	Tirane
_____	9. Slovakia	i.	Warsaw
_____	10. Slovenia	j.	Zagreb

81

Nicknames

Many places have nicknames in addition to their actual names. For example, Paris is known as "The City of Light." Chicago is known as "The Windy City." Sometimes these nicknames refer to some aspect of physical geography. Sometimes they refer to human characteristics, such as language, architecture, or music. Sometimes they refer to the economic activity of the city.

Look at the nicknames for the places shown below. For each one, decide whether it is based on physical geography (**P**), human characteristics (**H**), economic activity (**E**), or some other characteristic (**O**). Write the letter on the line provided before each city name.

City	Nickname
____ 1. Budapest, Hungary	City of Spas
____ 2. Dubrovnik, Croatia	The Pearl of the Adriatic
____ 3. Gdansk, Poland	World Capital of Amber
____ 4. Ljubljana, Slovenia	White Ljubljana
____ 5. Prague, Czech Republic	The City of a Hundred Spires

82

Popular Names in Poland

Some names are found in many different countries, but they can take slightly different forms. The names listed below are some of the most popular names in Poland. All of them are Polish versions of names that have other forms in the United States. How many of the Polish versions are you familiar with? How many of the U.S. versions can you identify? Write the U.S. version of each name on the line.

Boys

_____ 1. Andrzej

_____ 2. Jan

_____ 3. Józef

_____ 4. Krzysztof

_____ 5. Marek

_____ 6. Piotr

_____ 7. Pawel

Girls

_____ 8. Agnieszka

_____ 9. Elzbieta

_____ 10. Ewa

_____ 11. Katarzyna

_____ 12. Krystyna

_____ 13. Malgorzata

_____ 14. Zofia

83

Languages

Many of the languages of Eastern Europe are members of the Indo-European language family. However, other language groups in this area include the Uralic family as well as the Slavic, Baltic, and Illyric branches of Indo-European.

Many Slavic languages use the Cyrillic alphabet, but some use the Latin alphabet. The Uralic language family originated on the Siberian side of the Ural mountains. Several Uralic languages came to Europe over 1,500 years ago. The Baltic languages are found in the region near the Baltic Sea.

Some Eastern European languages are listed below. Decide if each one is a Uralic language (**U**), a Slavic language (**S**), a Baltic language (**B**), or is unrelated (**O**). Write the letter of the language division on the line before each language.

84

___ 1. Albanian

___ 2. Belarusian

___ 3. Bulgarian

___ 4. Croatian

___ 5. Czech

___ 6. Estonian

___ 7. Hungarian

___ 8. Macedonian

___ 9. Polish

___ 10. Russian

___ 11. Serbian

___ 12. Slovak

___ 13. Slovene

___ 14. Ukrainian

Population of Bulgaria

How has the population of Bulgaria changed over the last century? This table shows Bulgaria's population in different decades.

Use the figures to create a line graph that shows changes in the population of Bulgaria. Then answer the questions that follow.

Year	Population (in millions)
1900	3,744
1910	4,338
1920	4,847
1930	5,771
1940	6,536
1950	7,251
1960	7,857
1970	8,489
1980	8,877
1990	8,989
2000	8,150

Based on your graph, is the population of Bulgaria going up or down? What do you think has caused this trend upward or downward?

85

True or False?

Decide if each statement below is true (**T**) or false (**F**). Write the appropriate letter on the line before each statement. Rewrite any false statements to make them true.

____ 1. The mild climate of Eastern Europe is the result of warm winds off the Atlantic.

____ 2. The sandy beaches of Romania's Black Sea coast are popular vacation destinations.

____ 3. Moldova's location on the edge of the steppes of Central Asia has left it vulnerable to invasion.

____ 4. Thanks to its rich farmland, agricultural products are among Hungary's main exports.

____ 5. The borders of countries in Eastern Europe have been fixed since World War II.

86

What's the Question?

Each statement below is the answer to a question about the geography of Europe. For each one, write the original question.

1. the name for the former nation that broke apart into Slovenia, Croatia, Serbia and Montenegro, Macedonia, and Bosnia and Herzegovina

   _____

2. Europe's second-longest river that rises in Germany and flows through Austria, Slovakia, Hungary, Croatia, Serbia and Montenegro, Bulgaria, Romania, Moldova, and Ukraine

   _____

3. the landform separating Poland's plains from the Hungarian Basin region

   _____

4. the climate type, with warm summers, cold winters, and about 27 inches of annual precipitation, that covers the eastern part of Eastern Europe

   _____

87

Northern Eurasia Map

The map below shows part of Northern Eurasia, but no place names have been written on the map. Use your knowledge of the area to write each name where it belongs.

Countries	Cities
ARMENIA	Ashkhabad
AZERBAIJAN	Baku
GEORGIA	Tashkent
TURKMENISTAN	Tbilisi
UZBEKISTAN	Yerevan

88

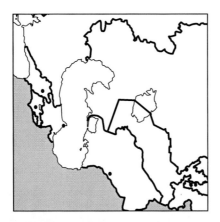

Absolute Location

Absolute location is the exact position on Earth where a place can be found. It is usually shown by using coordinates for latitude and longitude. No two places have the same absolute location.

Match each place named in the left column with its latitude and longitude in the right columns. Write the correct letter on the line.

Place		Latitude	Longitude
___ 1. Almaty, Kazakhstan	a.	69° 20' N	88° 6' E
___ 2. Baku, Azerbaijan	b.	43° 10' N	131° 53' E
___ 3. Norilsk, Russia	c.	43° 15' N	76° 57' E
___ 4. Samarkand, Uzbekistan	d.	40° 29' N	49° 56' E
___ 5. Vladivostok, Russia	e.	39° 40' N	66° 55' E

89

Relative Location

We can describe a place in relation to other places. This is called *relative location*. For each place named below, write a sentence that describes its location in relation to at least two other places.

Example: Moscow is northeast of Minsk and southeast of Tallinn.

1. Minsk is _____

    _____

2. Riga is _____

    _____

3. Kiev is _____

    _____

4. Tallinn is _____

    _____

90

Landforms

The map below shows some of the physical features of Kazakhstan. They include a lake, a desert, two mountain ranges, two rivers, and two seas. Label each one.

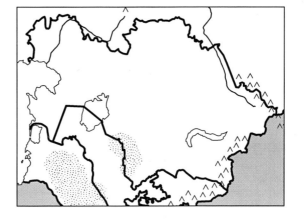

Facts About Northern Eurasia

How much do you know about the countries of Northern Eurasia? Choose one country from this region. Write its name at the top of the table below. Then fill in as much information as you can.

Country's name	
Relative location	
Primary language	
Primary religion	
Government	
Main industry	
Currency	

92

Countries and Capitals

Some Northern Eurasian countries and their capitals are listed below. Write the letter of the correct capital city on the line before each country.

	Country		Capital City
____ 1.	Armenia	a.	Alma-ata
____ 2.	Azerbaijan	b.	Baku
____ 3.	Belarus	c.	Bishkek
____ 4.	Estonia	d.	Dushanbe
____ 5.	Georgia	e.	Kiev
____ 6.	Kazakhstan	f.	Minsk
____ 7.	Kyrgyzstan	g.	Riga
____ 8.	Latvia	h.	Tallinn
____ 9.	Tajikistan	i.	Tbilisi
____ 10.	Ukraine	j.	Yerevan

93

Geography Terms

Each phrase below is the definition for a term used to describe the geography of Northern Eurasia. For each one, identify the term that is being defined. Write the term on the line.

_____ 1. the Russian word for fertile soil; it means "black earth"

_____ 2. a layer of soil just below Earth's surface that is frozen year-round

_____ 3. a cold, treeless plain where the only plants that grow there are dwarf shrubs, grasses, sedges, lichens, and mosses

94

_____ 4. a thinly scattered forest, dominated by spruce, fir, pine, and cedar; also called boreal forest

_____ 5. a semiarid grassy plain where few or no trees grow

Daily Warm-Ups: World Geography & Cultures

Population Distribution

The cities listed below are the nine largest cities in Northern Eurasia.

City	Population
Baku, Azerbaijan	2,100,000
Kharkov, Ukraine	1,500,000
Kiev, Ukraine	2,600,000
Minsk, Belarus	1,650,000
Moscow, Russia	10,500,000
Nizhni Novgorod, Russia	1,500,000
Novosibirsk, Russia	1,400,000
St. Petersburg, Russia	5,300,000
Tashkent, Uzbekistan	2,200,000

The location of these cities tells us something about the way population is distributed in the region. Think about where these cities are located. Answer the questions below.

1. What pattern of population distribution do you see? _____

   _____

2. Why do you think this distribution developed? _____

   _____

95

© 2006 Walch Publishing

Climate

Northern Eurasia covers a huge area. However, it has relatively few climate types. Write the letter of the correct climate type from the box on the line provided before each description below. (All temperatures and rainfall are averages.)

a.	arid	d.	subarctic
b.	humid continental	e.	tundra
c.	semiarid		

_____ 1. cold summers (40°F), very cold winters (0°F), yearly rainfall 16 inches

_____ 2. cool summers (56°F), very cold winters (−8°F), yearly rainfall 17 inches

_____ 3. warm summers (66°F), cold winters (21°F), yearly rainfall 27 inches

_____ 4. hot summers (78°F), mild to cold winters (51°F), yearly rainfall 18 inches

_____ 5. hot days, cold nights (summer 81°F, winter 55°F), yearly rainfall 5 inches

96

The Trans-Siberian Railroad

The Trans-Siberian Railroad is one of the most famous train routes in the world. Starting in Moscow and ending in Vladivostok, the main passenger route is 5,772 miles long. The train stops at a number of cities along the way, but most stops are less than 30 minutes long. The entire trip takes more than six days.

Think of a route that you often travel. It may be from your home to school, or somewhere you go for entertainment. Answer the following about your route.

1. Route: _____

2. Length (in miles): _____

3. How many times would you need to travel this route to cover the same distance as the Trans-Siberian Railroad? _____

4. If you travel this route twice a day (there and back), how many days would it take you to cover the distance of the Trans-Siberian Railroad? _____

97

Napoleon and Hitler

In 1812, France's Emperor Napoleon sent a huge army to attack Russia. The army reached Moscow and took the city. Within a few months, Napoleon's army was in ruins. Of the hundreds of thousands who marched into Russia, only a tiny fraction lived to return home.

In 1941, another European leader attacked Russia. This time, it was Germany's Adolf Hitler. Again, a huge army marched into Russia. Again, a number of cities fell to the invaders. And again, within a few months, the army was destroyed.

Russia's soldiers fought long and hard to defeat the invaders. But in both these wars, the Russian army had help from Russia's geography. What was it about Russia itself that helped defeat both invading armies? Write one or two sentences below for your answer.

98

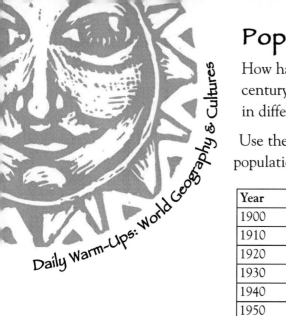

Population of Kazakhstan

How has the population of Kazakhstan changed over the last century? The table below gives figures for Kazakhstan's population in different decades.

Use the figures to create a line graph that shows changes in the population of Kazakhstan. Then answer the question that follows.

Year	Population (in millions)
1900	4,947
1910	5,982
1920	6,369
1930	6,096
1940	6,195
1950	6,703
1960	9,996
1970	13,009
1980	14,832
1990	16,690
2000	16,733

99

Based on the graph, what do you think the population of Kazakhstan will be in 2010? _____

Fill in the Blanks

Use your knowledge of the region to complete the paragraph about Siberia below.

Siberia, in northeastern Russia, is a vast lowland

_____. Its western edge is at the

_____ Mountains. In the east, it is bordered by the

_____ Ocean. The two major rivers of Siberia, the

_____ and the _____, rise in the

mountains to the south. They flow northward to the _____

Ocean. One of them begins near Lake _____, the world's

deepest freshwater lake. The intense cold of Siberia's _____ climate

has kept many people from settling there. In fact, much of the land there stays

frozen all year long.

100

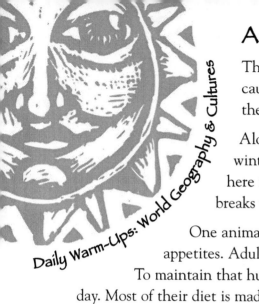

Arctic Life

The following passage about life in the Arctic describes several causes and effects. Read the passage. Circle the causes. Underline the effects. Draw a line to connect each cause and effect.

Along Russia's Arctic coast, the ground is frozen nearly all year. In winter, the ocean is blanketed with thick ice. The people who live here travel over the ice to fish and hunt. In summer, when the ice breaks up into huge chunks, or floes, they hunt from small boats.

One animal they hunt is the walrus. Walruses are huge animals, with huge appetites. Adult walruses weigh about 2,000 pounds and are about 10 feet long. To maintain that huge bulk, they eat about 5 percent of their total body weight per day. Most of their diet is made up of clams and other mollusks. To get at the clams, walruses use ice floes as bases from which they dive to the ocean floor.

Today, walrus populations in the Arctic are declining. Sea ice covers 15 percent less area than it did 20 years ago. The ice has thinned from 10 feet thick to less than 6 feet. Also, the ice is melting earlier in the year. The ice floes walruses use are no longer found near the shore, but are far from the coast in deeper waters. The walrus must dive deeper to look for food. Hunters must also travel farther out to sea in search of walruses, often returning empty-handed.

101

True or False?

Decide if each statement below is true (**T**) or false (**F**). Write the appropriate letter on the line before each statement. Rewrite any false statements to make them true.

____ 1. Most of Northern Eurasia was once part of the Russian Empire.

____ 2. The countries in this region are all about the same size.

____ 3. Many different languages and cultures are found in Northern Eurasia.

____ 4. The vast distances in Northern Eurasia affect the movement of both people and goods.

____ 5. Russia has few natural resources.

102

What's the Question?

Each statement below is the answer to a question about the geography of Northern Eurasia and Central Asia. For each one, write the original question.

1. the vast country, reaching from Europe to the Bering Sea, that still dominates the region

   _____

2. huge grassland plains that sweep across central Europe

   _____

3. the sea, bordered on the east by Ukraine, Russia, and Georgia, that lies between Europe and Central Asia

   _____

4. the largest area of unbroken lowland in the world, known for its long, harsh winters

   _____

103

Southwest Asia Map

The map below shows part of Southwest Asia, but no place-names have been written on the map. Use your knowledge of the area to write each name where it belongs.

Countries	Cities
KUWAIT	Abu Dhabi
OMAN	Doha
QATAR	Kuwait
SAUDI ARABIA	Muscat
UNITED ARAB EMIRATES	Riyadh
YEMEN	Sanaa

104

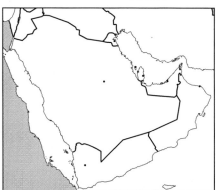

© 2006 Walch Publishing

Absolute Location

Absolute location is the exact position on Earth where a place can be found. It is usually shown by using coordinates for latitude and longitude. No two places have the same absolute location.

Match each place named in the left column with its latitude and longitude in the right columns. Write the correct letter on the line.

Place		Latitude	Longitude
___ 1.	Aden, Yemen	a. 38° 7' N	46° 20' E
___ 2.	Amman, Jordan	b. 12° 45' N	45° 0' E
___ 3.	Mecca, Saudi Arabia	c. 23° 37' N	58° 36' E
___ 4.	Muscat, Oman	d. 31° 57' N	35° 52' E
___ 5.	Tabriz, Iran	e. 21° 30' N	39° 34' E

105

Relative Location

We can describe a place in relation to other places. This is called *relative location*. For each place named below, write a sentence that describes its location in relation to at least two other places.

Example: Sanaa is southwest of Abu Dhabi and southeast of Nicosia.

1. Damascus is _____

   _____

2. Tehran is _____

   _____

3. Baghdad is _____

   _____

4. Ankara is _____

   _____

Landforms

The map below shows some of the physical features of Iran. They include one sea, two gulfs, two mountain ranges, two deserts, one river, and one strait. Label each one.

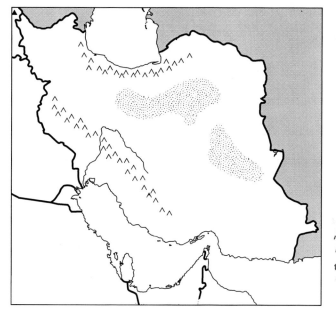

107

Islam

Founded in the early 600s C.E., Islam is an important aspect of the culture of Southwest Asia.

Islam has five basic tenets, called the Five Pillars of Islam. List the Five Pillars of Islam on the lines below.

1. _____

2. _____

3. _____

4. _____

5. _____

108

Facts About Southwest Asia

How much do you know about the countries of Southwest Asia? Choose one country from this region. Write its name at the top of the table below. Then fill in as much information as you can.

Country's name	
Relative location	
Primary language	
Primary religion	
Government	
Main industry	
Currency	

109

Countries and Capitals

Some Southwest Asian countries and their capitals are listed below. Write the letter of the correct capital city on the line before each country.

	Country		Capital City
_____ 1.	Bahrain	a.	Amman
_____ 2.	Cyprus	b.	Ankara
_____ 3.	Iran	c.	Baghdad
_____ 4.	Iraq	d.	Damascus
_____ 5.	Israel	e.	Jerusalem
_____ 6.	Jordan	f.	Manama
_____ 7.	Saudi Arabia	g.	Nicosía
_____ 8.	Syria	h.	Riyadh
_____ 9.	Turkey	i.	Sanaa
_____ 10.	Yemen	j.	Tehran

Daily Warm-Ups: World Geography & Cultures

Geography Terms

Each phrase below is the definition for a term used to describe the geography of Southwest Asia. For each one, identify the term that is being defined. Write the term on the line before the definition.

_____ 1. artificial watering of farmland, often through the use of canals

_____ 2. an area in a desert where a supply of freshwater allows plants to grow

_____ 3. a streambed in a desert region that is dry except during the rainy season

_____ 4. a seasonal wind shift that brings alternating wet and dry seasons

_____ 5. an area that receives less than 10 inches of rain a year, where few plants can grow

111

Nicknames

Many places have nicknames in addition to their actual names. For example, Paris is known as "The City of Light." Chicago is known as "The Windy City." Sometimes these nicknames refer to some aspect of physical geography. Sometimes they refer to human characteristics, such as language, architecture, or music. Sometimes they refer to the economic activity of the city.

Choose one of the cities listed below. Create a nickname that you think describes something about the city you chose. On the lines below, write the name of the city, your nickname for it, and one or two sentences explaining why you think the nickname fits the city.

Baghdad, Iraq

Beirut, Lebanon

Jeddah, Saudi Arabia

Jerusalem, Israel

Tehran, Iran

City: _____ Nickname: _____

Reason for nickname: _____

_____

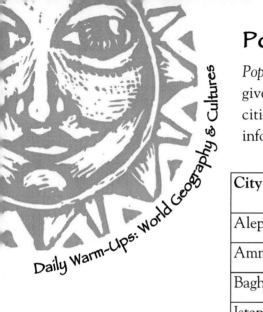

Population Density

Population density is the average number of people who live in a given area. The table below shows the population density for nine cities in Southwest Asia. Choose the best way to show this information in graph form. Then create your graph.

City	Population density (people per square mile)
Aleppo, Syria	25,900
Amman, Jordan	17,300
Baghdad, Iraq	23,900
Istanbul, Turkey	20,000
Jiddah, Saudi Arabia	9,200
Kabul, Afghanistan	37,100
Tehran, Iran	27,400
Tel Aviv, Israel	13,100
Riyadh, Saudi Arabia	9,400

113

© 2006 Walch Publishing

Population of Lebanon

How has the population of Lebanon changed over the last century? Accurate numbers are not available. The table below gives estimates for Lebanon's population in different decades.

Use the figures to create a line graph that shows changes in the population of Lebanon. Then answer the question that follows.

Year	Population (in millions)
1900	0.591
1910	0.707
1920	0.845
1930	1.010
1940	1.207
1950	1.443
1960	1.857
1970	2.469
1980	2.669
1990	2.740
2000	3.826

114

Based on the graph, what do you think the population of Lebanon will be in 2010? _____

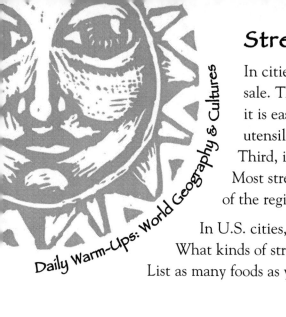

Street Food of Turkey

In cities all over the world, food vendors offer a variety of food for sale. The food they sell usually has a few things in common. First, it is easy to eat while on the go, either with fingers or simple utensils. Second, it is much cheaper than food in a restaurant. Third, it is ready right away, without needing any preparation time. Most street foods are also regional; they reflect the traditional food of the region.

In U.S. cities, common street foods include hot dogs and hamburgers. What kinds of street foods would you expect to find in the cities of Turkey? List as many foods as you can that meet the criteria described above.

115

True or False?

Decide if each statement below is true (**T**) or false (**F**). Write the appropriate letter on the line before each statement. Rewrite any false statements to make them true.

____ 1. Southwest Asia is also known as "the Middle East."

____ 2. Three continents—Asia, Africa, and Europe—come together in Southwest Asia.

____ 3. The borders of nations in this region have long been stable.

____ 4. Although three world religions began here, the region has seen little religious strife.

____ 5. The principal religion of Southwest Asia is Islam.

116

Daily Warm-Ups: World Geography & Cultures

One Region, Many Names

Some people call this region "Southwest Asia." Others know it as "the Middle East." Still others call this region "the Near East."

Why do you think there are so many different ways to refer to this region? Write two or three sentences for your answer.

117

What's the Question?

Each statement below is the answer to a question about the geography of Southwest Asia. For each one, write the original question on the line.

1. a vast desert plateau bounded on the north by Jordan and Iraq, on the east by the Persian Gulf and the Gulf of Oman, on the south by the Arabian Sea and the Gulf of Aden, and on the west by the Red Sea

   _____

2. a religion founded by Muhammad in the seventh century

   _____

3. the two rivers that were the site of one of the world's earliest civilizations

   _____

4. a naturally occurring substance made up of hydrocarbons

   _____

5. a nation formed after World War II as a homeland for Jews

   _____

118

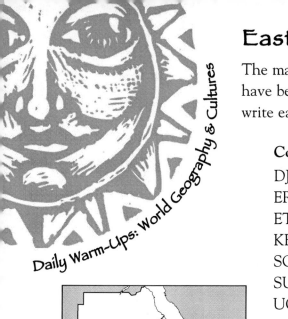

Daily Warm-Ups: World Geography & Cultures

East Africa Map

The map below shows part of East Africa, but no place-names have been written on the map. Use your knowledge of the area to write each name where it belongs.

Countries	Cities
DJIBOUTI	Addis Ababa
ERITREA	Asmara
ETHIOPIA	Djibouti
KENYA	Kampala
SOMALIA	Khartoum
SUDAN	Mogadishu
UGANDA	Nairobi

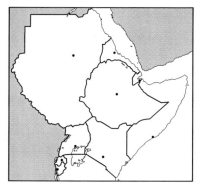

119

© 2006 Walch Publishing

Absolute Location

Absolute location is the exact position on Earth where a place can be found. It is usually shown by using coordinates for latitude and longitude. No two places have the same absolute location.

Match each place named in the left column with its latitude and longitude in the right columns. Write the correct letter on the line.

	Place		Latitude	Longitude
___ 1.	Douala, Cameroon	a.	4° 2' S	39° 43' E
___ 2.	Khartoum, Sudan	b.	12° 10' N	14° 59' E
___ 3.	Mogadishu, Somalia	c.	4° 0' N	9° 45' E
___ 4.	Mombasa, Kenya	d.	15° 31' N	32° 35' E
___ 5.	Ndjamena, Chad	e.	2° 2' N	45° 25' E

120

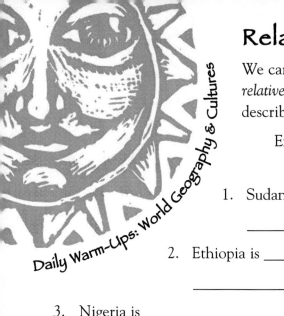

Relative Location

We can describe a place in relation to other places. This is called *relative location*. For each place named below, write a sentence that describes its location in relation to at least two other places.

Example: Libya is northeast of Mali and west of Egypt.

1. Sudan is _____

    _____

2. Ethiopia is _____

    _____

3. Nigeria is _____

    _____

4. Kenya is _____

    _____

121

Landforms

The map below shows some of the physical features of Sudan. They include one important river and its two major tributaries, one desert, and one sea. Label each one.

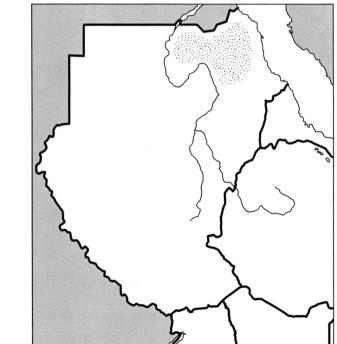

122

Regions

Africa is a huge geographic area. Within this larg[e]
different regions can be identified. Name three [c]
For each one, name at least three countries with[in]

Region 1: _____

    Country 1: _____

    Country 2: _____

    Country 3: _____

Region 2: _____

    Country 1: _____

    Country 2: _____

    Country 3: _____

Region 3: _____

    Country 1: _____

    Country 2: _____

    Country 3: _____

123

ders and Boundaries

ng the 1800s, European countries took control of much of
rica. They divided the continent into colonies. However, the
orders they chose often had nothing to do with the African
people who lived in different regions.

This policy caused many problems in Africa. Some of them still
affect African nations today. Write a paragraph describing some of
these problems and their continuing effects.

124

Colonial Rule

The European countries in the box once ruled much of Africa. Which colonial power once controlled each African nation listed below? Write the letter of the correct colonial power on the line before each name.

a. Belgium	c. France	e. Portugal
b. Britain	d. Germany	

_____ 1. Algeria

_____ 2. Angola

_____ 3. Botswana

_____ 4. Cameroon

_____ 5. Democratic Republic of the Congo

_____ 6. Ivory Coast

_____ 7. Kenya

_____ 8. Mali

_____ 9. Morocco

_____ 10. Mozambique

_____ 11. Namibia

_____ 12. Niger

_____ 13. Senegal

_____ 14. South Africa

_____ 15. Sudan

_____ 16. Tanzania

_____ 17. Tunisia

_____ 18. Uganda

_____ 19. Zambia

_____ 20. Zimbabwe

125

The Nile River

The graph below shows the average amount of water that flows through the Nile River every month. Look carefully at the graph. What inference about the river can you make, based on the graph?

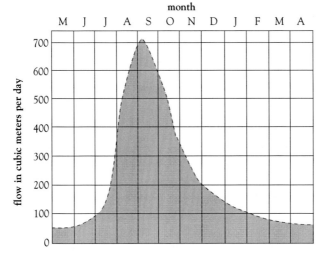

126

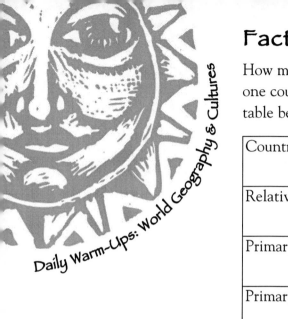

Facts About Africa

How much do you know about the countries of Africa? Choose one country from this region. Write its name at the top of the table below. Then fill in as much information as you can.

Country's name	
Relative location	
Primary language	
Primary religion	
Government	
Main industry	
Currency	

127

Countries and Capitals

Some African countries and their capitals are listed below. Write the letter of the correct city on the line before each country.

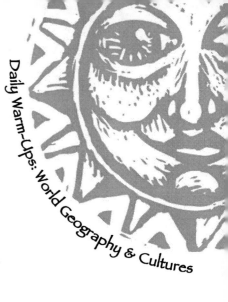

	Country		Capital City
____ 1.	Algeria	a.	Algiers
____ 2.	Botswana	b.	Bamako
____ 3.	Chad	c.	Cairo
____ 4.	Egypt	d.	Dar es Salaam
____ 5.	Kenya	e.	Gaborone
____ 6.	Mali	f.	Mogadishu
____ 7.	Namibia	g.	Nairobi
____ 8.	Niger	h.	N'Djamena
____ 9.	Somalia	i.	Niamey
____ 10.	Tanzania	j.	Windhoek

128

Population Distribution

The cities below, listed in order of population, are the fifteen largest cities in Africa.

Lagos, Nigeria

Cairo, Egypt

Kinshasa, Democratic Republic of the Congo

Alexandria, Egypt

Casablanca, Morocco

Abidjan, Ivory Coast

Kano, Nigeria

Ibadan, Nigeria

Cape Town, South Africa

Addis Ababa, Ethiopia

Giza, Egypt

Nairobi, Kenya

Dar es Salaam, Tanzania

Dakar, Senegal

Durban, South Africa

The location of these cities tells something about the way population is distributed in the region. Think about where these cities are located.

1. What pattern of population distribution do you see? _____

   _____

2. Why do you think this distribution developed? _____

   _____

129

© 2006 Walch Publishing

Nicknames

Many places have nicknames in addition to their actual names. For example, Paris is known as "The City of Light." Chicago is known as "The Windy City." Sometimes these nicknames refer to some aspect of physical geography. Sometimes they refer to human characteristics, such as language, architecture, or music. Sometimes they refer to the economic activity of the city.

Choose one of the cities listed below. Create a nickname that you think describes something about the city you chose. On the lines below, write the name of the city, your nickname for it, and one or two sentences explaining why you think the nickname fits the city.

Addis Ababa, Ethiopia

Alexandria, Egypt

Khartoum, Sudan

Bangui, Central African Republic

130

City: _____ Nickname: _____

Reason for nickname: _____

_____

Population Density

Population density is the average number of people living in a given area. The table below shows the population density and area of some cities in Africa. For some cities, the population density has been calculated. Use the information you have been given to calculate the population density of the remaining cities, and fill it in on the table below. Round to the nearest hundred.

City	Population	Area (sq. mi.)	Population density per sq. mi.
Abidjan, Ivory Coast	3,300,000	115	28,700
Cairo, Egypt	12,200,000	500	_____
Conakry, Guinea	1,300,000	62	_____
Khartoum, Sudan	4,000,000	225	_____
Kinshasa, Democratic Republic of the Congo	5,000,000	181	27,600
Nairobi, Kenya	2,000,000	90	_____

131

Changes in the Environment

For thousands of years, people have adapted their environments to fit their needs. This can include cutting down trees; plowing fields; moving rocks; erecting buildings; building roads, bridges, and tunnels; and more.

Choose a place in Africa where people have modified their environment. List all the ways in which the environment has been changed to meet the needs of the people who live there.

Place: _____

Changes: _____

_____

_____

_____

_____

_____

132

Population of the Democratic Republic of the Congo

How has the population of the Democratic Republic of the Congo (DRC) changed over the last century? The table below gives figures for the DRC's population in different decades. The figure for 2010 is an estimate.

Use the figures to create a line graph that shows changes in the population of the DRC. Then answer the question that follows.

Year	Population (in millions)
1900	4,103
1910	5,101
1920	6,341
1930	7,884
1940	10,356
1950	11,203
1960	14,169
1970	21,688
1980	27,009
1990	37,391
2000	51,965
2010 (est)	67,930

Based on your graph, what do you think the population of the DRC will be in 2020?

_____

133

True or False?

Decide if each statement below is true (**T**) or false (**F**). Write the appropriate letter on the line before each statement. Rewrite any false statements to make them true.

____ 1. Most large African cities are either on the coast or on a river.

____ 2. The equator passes through the southern tip of Egypt.

____ 3. Monroeville, the capital of Liberia, was named for a U.S. president.

134

____ 4. Eritrea was one of the first independent nations in Africa.

____ 5. The Sahara Desert separates North Africa from the rest of the continent.

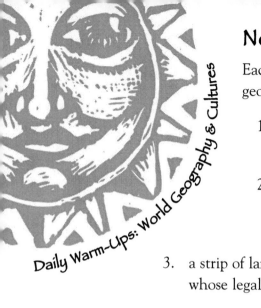

North Africa: What's the Question?

Each statement below is the answer to a question about the geography of Africa. For each one, write the original question.

1. the vast desert area that covers much of North Africa

   _____

2. the river, more than 4,000 miles long, that flows north through Egypt to the Mediterranean Sea

   _____

3. a strip of land on the west coast of North Africa, claimed by Morocco, whose legal status is unresolved

   _____

4. the largest country in North Africa, bordered by Morocco in the west and Tunisia and Libya in the east

   _____

5. the process through which a desert spreads to a non-desert area

   _____

135

West and Central Africa: What's the Question?

Each statement below is the answer to a question about the geography of Africa. For each one, write the original question.

1. a wide band of semiarid land that separates the deserts of North Africa and the savanna to the south

    _____

2. the destruction of forests through human activity

    _____

136

3. also known as the Zaire River, the largest river of the region and the second-longest in Africa after the Nile

    _____

4. the main crop of West Africa, often processed for sweet snacks or beverages

    _____

5. the West African nation whose rich oil reserves provide much of its income

    _____

South Asia Map

The map below shows part of South Asia, but no place-names have been written on the map. Use your knowledge of the area to write each name where it belongs.

Countries	Cities
BANGLADESH	Dhaka
BHUTAN	Kathmandu
NEPAL	Thimphu

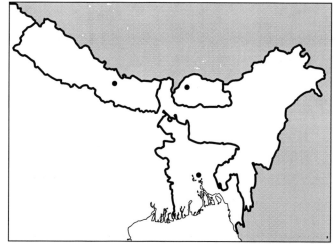

137

Absolute Location

Absolute location is the exact position on Earth where a place can be found. It is usually shown by using coordinates for latitude and longitude. No two places have the same absolute location.

Match each place named in the left column with its latitude and longitude in the right columns. Write the correct letter on the line.

	Place		Latitude	Longitude
___ 1.	Bangalore, India	a.	27° 31' N	89° 45' E
___ 2.	Colombo, Sri Lanka	b.	12° 59' N	77° 40' E
___ 3.	Dhaka, Bangladesh	c.	24° 53' N	67° 0' E
___ 4.	Karachi, Pakistan	d.	6° 56' N	79° 58' E
___ 5.	Thimphu, Bhutan	e.	23° 43' N	90° 26' E

138

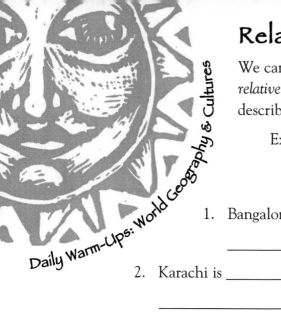

Relative Location

We can describe a place in relation to other places. This is called *relative location*. For each place named below, write a sentence that describes its location in relation to at least two other places.

Example: Calcutta is southeast of Kathmandu and northeast of Bangalore.

1. Bangalore is _____
   _____

2. Karachi is _____
   _____

3. Dhaka is _____
   _____

4. Kabul is _____
   _____

139

Landforms

The map below shows some of the physical features of Pakistan. They include one major river and its main tributary, two mountain ranges, one desert, and one sea. Label each one.

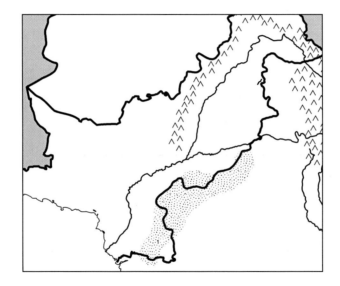

140

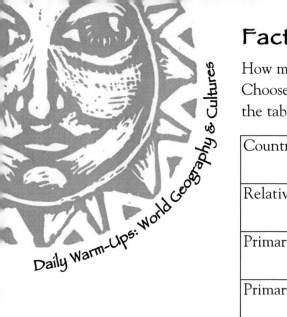

Facts About South Asia

How much do you know about the countries of South Asia? Choose one country from this region. Write its name at the top of the table below. Then fill in as much information as you can.

Country's name	
Relative location	
Primary language	
Primary religion	
Government	
Main industry	
Currency	

141

Countries and Capitals

Some South Asian countries and their capitals are listed below.
Write the letter of the correct capital city on the line provided
before each country.

	Country		Capital City
_____ 1.	Afghanistan	a.	Colombo
_____ 2.	Bangladesh	b.	Dhaka
_____ 3.	Bhutan	c.	Islamabad
_____ 4.	India	d.	Kabul
_____ 5.	Nepal	e.	Kathmandu
_____ 6.	Pakistan	f.	New Delhi
_____ 7.	Sri Lanka	g.	Thimphu

142

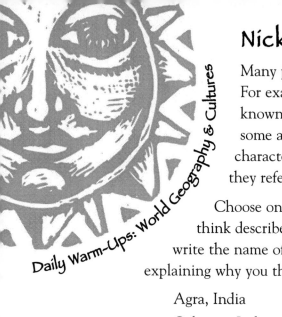

Nicknames

Many places have nicknames in addition to their actual names. For example, Paris is known as "The City of Light." Chicago is known as "The Windy City." Sometimes these nicknames refer to some aspect of physical geography. Sometimes they refer to human characteristics, such as language, architecture, or music. Sometimes they refer to the economic activity of the city.

Choose one of the cities listed below. Create a nickname that you think describes something about the city you chose. On the lines below, write the name of the city, your nickname for it, and one or two sentences explaining why you think the nickname fits the city.

Agra, India   Karachi, Pakistan

Calcutta, India   Lahore, Pakistan

Dhaka, Bangladesh   Madras, India

Islamabad, Pakistan   Thimphu, Bhutan

143

City: _____ Nickname: _____

Reason for nickname: _____

_____

Population Density

Population density is the average number of people who live in a given area. The graph below shows the population density of some cities in South Asia. Study the graph. Then answer the questions.

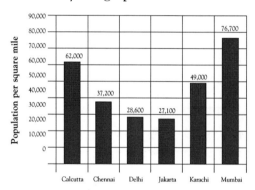

Population per square mile

Calcutta	62,000
Chennai	37,200
Delhi	28,600
Jakarta	27,100
Karachi	49,000
Mumbai	76,700

144

1. Which is the most densely populated city on the graph? _____

2. The most densely populated city in the United States is San Jose, California, with about 5,900 people per square mile. How does this compare to the cities on the graph? _____

   _____

3. What might be some advantages and disadvantages of living in a densely populated city? List as many of both as you can. _____

Population of India

How has the population of India changed since the country became independent? The table below gives figures for India's population in different decades. The figure for 2010 is an estimate.

Use the figures to create a line graph that shows changes in the population of India.

Year	Population (in millions)
1950	369,880
1960	445,857
1970	555,043
1980	692,394
1990	855,591
2000	1,012,909
2010 (est.)	1,155,830

145

Street Food of India

In cities all over the world, food vendors offer a variety of food for sale. The food they sell usually has a few things in common. First, it is easy to eat while on the go, either with fingers or simple utensils. Second, it is much cheaper than food in a restaurant. Third, it is ready right away, without needing any preparation time. Most street foods are also regional; they reflect the traditional food of the region.

In U.S. cities, common street foods include hot dogs and hamburgers. What kinds of street foods would you expect to find in the cities of India? Name as many foods as you can that meet the criteria described above.

146

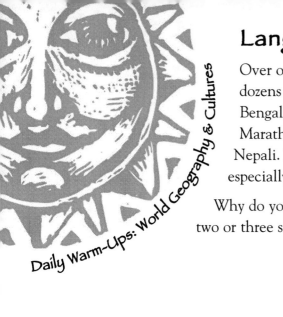

Languages of India

Over one billion people live in India. Among them, they speak dozens of languages. India's official languages include Assamese, Bengali, Gujarati, Hindi, Kannarese, Kashmiri, Malayalam, Marathi, Oriya, Punjabi, Sanskrit, Tamil, Telugu, Urdu, and Nepali. English is not an official language, but it is often used, especially in business communication.

Why do you think one country has so many different languages? Write two or three sentences for your answer.

147

True or False?

Decide if each statement below is true (**T**) or false (**F**). Write the appropriate letter on the line before each statement. Rewrite any false statements to make them true.

____ 1. South Asia is one of the most densely populated areas of the world.

____ 2. In most parts of South Asia, the climate is the same all year-round.

____ 3. Some of the world's tallest mountains are found in South Asia.

____ 4. Much of South Asia was once under British rule.

____ 5. Conflicts between Muslims and Hindus have caused much tension in South Asia.

148

What's the Question?

Each statement below is the answer to a question about the geography of South Asia. For each one, write the original question.

1. the highest mountain range in the world, separating South Asia and the rest of Asia

    _____

2. a seasonal shift in the prevailing winds that brings alternating wet and dry seasons

    _____

3. the largest country in South Asia

    _____

4. the predominantly Muslim country formed when India gained its independence from Britain

    _____

5. an island nation in the Indian Ocean, formerly called Ceylon

    _____

149

East Asia Map

The map below shows part of East Asia, but no place-names have been written on the map. Use your knowledge of the area to write each name where it belongs.

Countries	Cities
CAMBODIA	Bangkok
LAOS	Hanoi
MYANMAR (BURMA)	Phnom Penh
THAILAND	Vientiane
VIETNAM	Yangon (Rangoon)

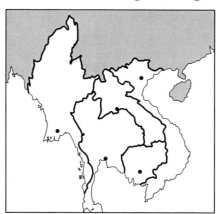

Absolute Location

Absolute location is the exact position on Earth where a place can be found. It is usually shown by using coordinates for latitude and longitude. No two places have the same absolute location.

Match each place on the left with its latitude and longitude on the right. Write the correct letter on the line.

Place		Latitude	Longitude
___ 1. Bandar Seri Begawan, Brunei	a.	34° 40' N	135° 30' E
___ 2. Lhasa, China	b.	4° 52' N	115° 0' E
___ 3. Luzon, Philippines	c.	47° 55' N	106° 53' E
___ 4. Osaka, Japan	d.	16° 0' N	121° 0' E
___ 5. Ulan Bator, Mongolia	e.	29° 25' N	90° 58' E

151

Relative Location

We can describe a place in relation to other places. This is called *relative location*. For each place named below, write a sentence that describes its location in relation to at least two other places.

Example: Beijing is southeast of Ulan Bator and northwest of Taipei.

1. Bangkok is _____
_____

2. Hong Kong is _____
_____

3. Seoul is _____
_____

4. Tokyo is _____
_____

152

Landforms

The map below shows some of the physical features of Mongolia. They include one desert and two mountain ranges. Label each one. *Bonus:* Can you also label the countries that border Mongolia on the north and south?

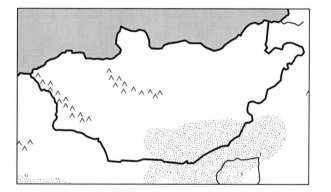

or starved to death. This helped the Russian army defeat the invading armies.

99.

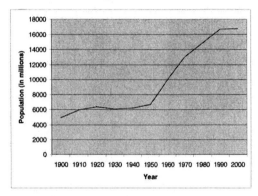

Answers will vary. Sample answer: 19,627 million

100. 1. plain; 2. Ural; 3. Pacific; 4. Lena; 5. Yenisei; 6. Arctic; 7. Baikal; 8. subarctic

101. Cause: In winter, the ocean is blanketed with thick ice.
Effect: The people who live here travel over the ice to fish and hunt.

Cause: In summer, the ice breaks up into huge chunks.
Effect: They hunt from small boats.
Cause: Adult walruses weigh about 2,000 pounds and are about 10 feet long.
Effect: To maintain that huge bulk, they eat about 5 percent of their total body weight per day.
Cause: Most of their diet is made up of clams and other mollusks.
Effect: To get at the clams, walruses use ice floes as bases from which they dive to the ocean floor.
Cause: The ice floes walruses use are no longer found near the shore, but are far from the coast in deeper waters.
Effect: The walrus must dive deeper to look for food.
Cause: Walrus populations in the Arctic are declining.
Effect: Hunters must also travel farther out to sea in search of walruses, often returning empty-handed.

Facts About East Asia

How much do you know about the countries of East Asia? Choose one country from this region. Write its name at the top of the table below. Then fill in as much information as you can.

Country's name	
Relative location	
Primary language	
Primary religion	
Government	
Main industry	
Currency	

154

Countries and Capitals

Some East Asian countries and their capitals are listed below. Write the letter of the correct capital city on the line before each country.

		Country		Capital City
____	1.	Cambodia	a.	Bangkok
____	2.	China	b.	Beijing
____	3.	Japan	c.	Hanoi
____	4.	Laos	d.	Phnom Penh
____	5.	Mongolia	e.	Pyongyang
____	6.	Myanmar (Burma)	f.	Seoul
____	7.	North Korea	g.	Taipei
____	8.	South Korea	h.	Tokyo
____	9.	Taiwan	i.	Ulan Bator
____	10.	Thailand	j.	Vientiane
____	11.	Vietnam	k.	Yangon

155

Geography Terms

Each phrase below is the definition for a term used to describe the geography of East Asia. For each one, identify the term that is being defined. Write the term on the line before the definition.

_____ 1. the fertile soil made up of small particles transported by the wind

_____ 2. a small plot of land that can be flooded for growing rice

_____ 3. a zone of instability in Earth's crust along the boundaries of tectonic plates, marked by earthquakes and volcanic activity, that rings the Pacific Ocean basin

_____ 4. a naturally occurring opening in Earth's surface through which molten, solid, and gaseous materials erupt

_____ 5. a wind system that changes direction seasonally, creating wet and dry seasons

156

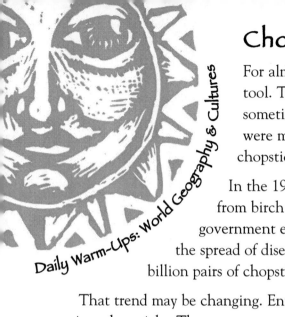

Chopsticks

For almost 4,000 years, chopsticks have been China's main eating tool. Traditionally, they were carved from wood or bamboo, sometimes lacquered, sometimes plain. More expensive chopsticks were made of ivory or metal, including silver and gold. These chopsticks were washed after a meal and reused.

In the 1980s, disposable chopsticks were introduced in China. Made from birch or poplar, they were cheap and convenient. The Chinese government encouraged the use of disposable chopsticks as a way to fight the spread of diseases. By 2005, China used—and threw away—more than 45 billion pairs of chopsticks every year.

That trend may be changing. Environmentalists now urge people to stop using one-time chopsticks. The government has imposed a new tax on disposable items, including chopsticks.

Why do you think environmentalists and the government want to stop the use of disposable chopsticks? Write two or three sentences for your answer.

157

Population Density

Population density is the average number of people living in a given area. The graph below shows the population density of some cities in East Asia. Study the graph. Then answer the questions that follow.

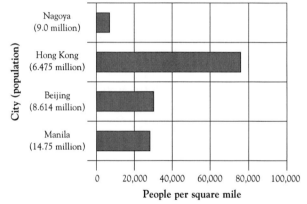

158

1. Which city on the graph has the largest population? _____

2. Which city on the graph has the greatest population density?

    _____

3. Why do you think the population here is so dense? _____

    _____

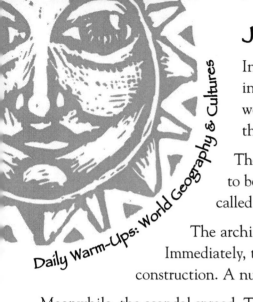

Japan's Building Scandal

In 2005, a building scandal rocked Japan. It started with a building inspection company's internal review of approved designs by a well-known architect. The review showed that some of the designs the company had approved used faked figures.

The architect's job included calculating the amount of reinforced steel to be used in new buildings. On at least 21 buildings, the architect called for too few steel bars, or bars that were too thin—or both.

The architect admitted that he had falsified the figures on his designs. Immediately, the authorities stopped work on a number of buildings under construction. A number of buildings were ordered to be demolished.

Meanwhile, the scandal spread. The architect said building contractors had pressured him to reduce the amount of steel in his designs. He pointed out that inspectors had approved the plans with faked figures. People called for a thorough investigation. The Japanese government announced that it would do strength tests on every condominium complex in the country.

Why do you think one architect's failure to require enough steel bars in his designs prompted such a reaction?

159

Changes in the Environment

For thousands of years, people have adapted their environments to fit their needs. This can include cutting down trees; plowing fields; moving rocks; erecting buildings; building roads, bridges, and tunnels; and more.

Choose a place in East Asia where people have modified their environment. List all the ways in which the environment has been changed to meet the needs of the people who live there.

Place: _____

Changes: _____

_____

_____

_____

_____

_____

160

Regions of China

The People's Republic of China covers a huge geographic area. Within this large area, many different regions can be identified. Name two of China's regions. For each one, describe its boundaries and the shared characteristics of places within the region.

Region 1: _____

_____

_____

Region 2: _____

_____

_____

161

Street Food of China

In cities all over the world, food vendors offer a variety of food for sale. The food they sell usually has a few things in common. First, it is easy to eat while on the go, either with fingers or simple utensils. Second, it is much cheaper than food in a restaurant. Third, it is ready right away, without needing any preparation time. Most street foods are also regional; they reflect the traditional food of the region.

In U.S. cities, common street foods include hot dogs and hamburgers. What kinds of street foods would you expect to find in the cities of China? Name as many foods as you can that meet the criteria described above.

162

Population of China

How has the population of China changed over the last century? The table below gives figures for China's population in different decades. The figure for 2010 is an estimate.

Use the figures to create a line graph that shows changes in the population of China. Then answer the question that follows.

Year	Population (in millions)
1900	400,000
1910	423,000
1920	472,000
1930	489,000
1940	520,843
1950	556,613
1960	682,024
1970	825,812
1980	981,200
1990	1,133,682
2000	1,265,830
2010 (est)	1,347,514

To control population growth, China introduced a "one child" policy in 1979. With a few exceptions, each couple living in a city should have only one child. In most rural areas, a couple may have a second child a few years after the first child is born. Based on your graph, do you think this policy is working to control population growth? Explain your answer.

163

True or False?

Decide if each statement below is true (**T**) or false (**F**). Write the appropriate letter on the line before each statement. Rewrite any false statements to make them true.

____ 1. China's Yellow River is an important resource, but it has also caused great destruction.

____ 2. Japan's location near mainland Asia means it rarely suffers from extreme weather.

____ 3. Although China still has a communist government, its economy has become more capitalist in recent years.

____ 4. North Korea and South Korea are separate countries, but their culture, economy, and government are very similar.

____ 5. Tibet, in China's southwest, is largely made up of a huge, high plateau.

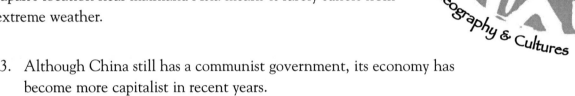

164

What's the Question?

Each statement below is the answer to a question about the geography of East Asia. For each one, write the original question.

1. the largest nation in East Asia, and the site of one of the world's earliest civilizations

   _____

2. an island, now part of the People's Republic of China, that was a British colony until 1997

   _____

3. a sudden, violent movement of Earth's crust causing great damage

   _____

4. an important food crop in much of East Asia, grown in flooded fields called *paddies*

   _____

5. a high-protein East Asian legume used to make tofu, miso, and other foods

   _____

165

Australia and New Zealand Map

The map below shows Australia, New Zealand, and the Pacific World, but no place-names have been written on the map. Use your knowledge of the area to write each name where it belongs.

Countries	Cities	
AUSTRALIA	Adelaide	Melbourne
NEW ZEALAND	Brisbane	Perth
	Canberra	Sydney
	Darwin	Wellington
	Hobart	

166

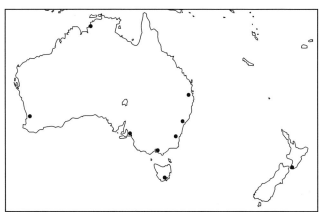

Absolute Location

Absolute location is the exact position on Earth where a place can be found. It is usually shown by using coordinates for latitude and longitude. No two places have the same absolute location.

Match each place named in the left column with its latitude and longitude in the right columns. Write the correct letter on the line.

	Place		Latitude	Longitude
___ 1.	Auckland	a.	15° 0' S	168° 0' E
___ 2.	Melbourne	b.	36° 52' S	174° 46' E
___ 3.	Nouméa, New Caledonia	c.	22° 17' S	166° 30' E
___ 4.	Vanuatu	d.	37° 50' S	145° 0' E

167

Relative Location

We can describe a place in relation to other places. This is called *relative location*. For each place named below, write a sentence that describes its location in relation to at least two other places.

Example: Perth is northwest of Melbourne and southwest of Nouméa.

1. Adelaide is _____

   _____

2. Canberra is _____

   _____

3. Nouméa is _____

   _____

4. Wellington is _____

   _____

168

Landforms

The map below shows some of the physical features of Australia. They include two deserts, two mountain ranges, three rivers that merge into one, one lake, and an underwater reef. Label each one.

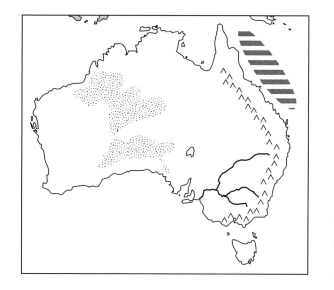

Facts About Australia, New Zealand, and the Pacific World

How much do you know about the countries of Australia, New Zealand, and the Pacific World? Choose one country from this region. Write its name at the top of the table below. Then fill in as much information as you can.

170

Country's name	
Relative location	
Primary language	
Primary religion	
Government	
Main industry	
Currency	

Countries and Capitals

Some countries and their capitals are listed below. Write the letter of the correct capital city on the line before each country.

Country		Capital City
___ 1. Australia	a.	Bairiki
___ 2. Brunei	b.	Bandar Seri Begawan
___ 3. Federated States of Micronesia	c.	Canberra
___ 4. Fiji	d.	Honiara
___ 5. Kiribati	e.	Nuku'alafa
___ 6. New Zealand	f.	Palikir
___ 7. Papua New Guinea	g.	Port Moresby
___ 8. Solomon Islands	h.	Port Vila
___ 9. Tonga	i.	Suva
___ 10. Vanuatu	j.	Wellington

171

Geography Terms

Each phrase below is the definition for a term used to describe the geography of Australia, New Zealand, and the Pacific World. For each one, identify the term that is being defined. Write the term on the line before the definition.

_____ 1. a marine ridge, found in the shallow coastal water of warm oceans, made up of the exterior skeletons of colonies of tiny marine animals

_____ 2. a ring-shaped island or group of islands, common in the Pacific Ocean

_____ 3. a chain or set of islands, grouped together

_____ 4. a tropical storm of the Pacific Ocean that has winds of at least 74 miles per hour; known as a hurricane in the Atlantic Ocean

_____ 5. a wave or series of waves in a body of water caused by a sudden disturbance that displaces water, such as an underwater earthquake; can be devastating to low-lying areas

172

Daily Warm-Ups: World Geography & Cultures

Colonies

Many island groups in the Pacific are still colonies of other nations. Choose the colonial power from the box that rules each island group below. Write the letter of the correct colonial power on the line before each island group.

a. France	b. United Kingdom	c. United States

Island or Island Group

____ 1. American Samoa

____ 2. Baker Island

____ 3. French Polynesia

____ 4. Guam

____ 5. New Caledonia

____ 6. Pitcairn Islands

____ 7. Wallis and Futuna

173

Tuvalu

Tuvalu is a tiny island nation in the South Pacific, halfway between Australia and Hawaii. It consists of nine coral atolls, with poor soil and no known mineral resources. The highest point on the islands is just 15 feet above sea level.

Despite the lack of resources on Tuvalu, the islands are densely populated. About 11,000 people live on the islands' 10 square miles of land.

Once a British colony, the nation became independent in 1978. Today, Tuvalu's future is at risk. The government of Tuvalu has set up an evacuation plan with Australia and New Zealand in case the entire population needs to be relocated.

Based on what you know about global changes and the geography of Tuvalu, what danger do you think threatens the nation? Write your answer below.

174

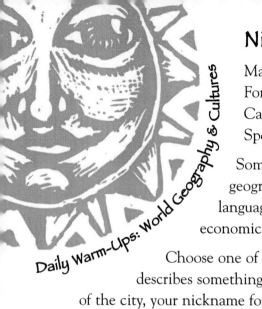

Nicknames

Many places have nicknames in addition to their actual names. For example, Canberra, Australia, is known as "The Bush Capital." Queenstown, New Zealand, is known as the "Extreme Sports Capital of the World."

Sometimes these nicknames refer to some aspect of physical geography. Sometimes they refer to human characteristics, such as language, architecture, or music. Sometimes they refer to the economic activity of the city.

Choose one of the cities listed below. Create a nickname that you think describes something about the city you chose. On the lines below, write the name of the city, your nickname for it, and one or two sentences explaining why you think the nickname fits the city you chose.

Adelaide, Australia   Nouméa, New Caledonia   Sydney, Australia

Auckland, New Zealand   Perth, Australia   Te Puke, New Zealand

Brisbane, Australia

City: _____   Nickname: _____

Reason for nickname: _____

175

Population of Australia

How has the population of Australia changed over the last century? The table below gives figures for Australia's population in different decades.

Use the figures to create a line graph that shows changes in the population of Australia. Then answer the question that follows.

Year	Population (in millions)
1900	3,765
1910	4,525
1920	5,411
1930	6,501
1940	7,078
1950	8,307
1960	10,392
1970	12,663
1980	14,726
1990	17,169
2000	19,169

176

Based on the graph, what do you think the population of Australia will be in 2010? _____

Population Distribution

The cities listed below are the largest cities in Australia.

City	Population
Adelaide	1,002,000
Brisbane	1,508,000
Canberra	325,000
Geelong	130,000
Gosford	255,000
Melbourne	3,162,000
Newcastle	280,000
Perth	1,177,000
Sydney	3,502,000
Wollongong	229,000

The location of these cities tells us something about the way population is distributed in Australia. Think about where these cities are located. Answer the questions on the lines.

1. What pattern of population distribution do you see? _____

_____

2. Why do you think this distribution developed? _____

_____

177

True or False?

Decide if each statement below is true (**T**) or false (**F**). Write the appropriate letter on the line before each statement. Rewrite any false statements to make them true.

____ 1. Australia and New Zealand were French colonies until the early 1900s.

____ 2. The mountains of Australia's Great Dividing Range keep rain from reaching most of the country's interior.

____ 3. Raising livestock is an important part of Australia's economy.

____ 4. New Zealand's mild climate and plentiful rainfall make it good farming country.

____ 5. In most Pacific islands, farming is the mainstay of the economy.

178

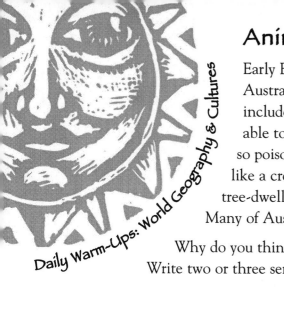

Animals of Australia

Early European settlers were amazed by the animals they saw in Australia—animals no westerner had ever seen before. They included emus and cassowaries, huge birds that do not fly but are able to run at extraordinary speeds. Some Australian jellyfish are so poisonous that one sting can kill a person. The platypus looks like a cross between a duck and a mole. Kangaroos range from tiny tree-dwellers to the red kangaroo, which can weigh up to 200 pounds. Many of Australia's animals are found nowhere else in the world.

Why do you think so many unique animal species are found in Australia? Write two or three sentences for your answer below.

179

What's the Question?

Each statement below is the answer to a question about the geography of Australia, New Zealand, and the Pacific World. For each one, write the original question.

1. the original people of New Zealand, who probably first arrived in New Zealand in canoes from other islands

   _____

2. the imaginary line at 180° that separates two calendar days

   _____

3. a valuable source of fertilizer that was once an important part of Nauru's economy but that has now been almost mined out

   _____

4. the world's southernmost continent, almost entirely covered in ice, with no permanent population

   _____

5. a ring-shaped island or group of islands

   _____

180

1. Answers will vary. Sample answers: 1. Africa is southwest of East Asia and northwest of Australia. 2. Southwest Asia is northeast of Africa and northwest of Australia. 3. North America is northwest of South America and east of East Asia. 4. East Asia is northeast of Africa and west of North America.

2. Answers will vary, but should show appropriate use of the scale on the map.

3.

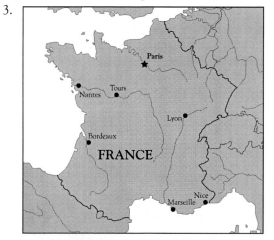

4. 1. L; 2. M; 3. L; 4. M; 5. C; 6. M; 7. C; 8. L; 9. C

5.

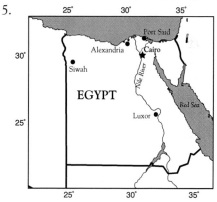

6. 1. b; 2. a; 3. e; 4. c; 5. d

7. Answers will vary.

8. Answers will vary. Sample answer: No, the population in Tanzania will be much larger, and in Poland it will be much smaller. Since 44% of the population in Tanzania is under the age of 15, this means that many Tanzanian women are just

Daily Warm-Ups: World Geography & Cultures

reaching childbearing age. On average, each of these women will have 5.06 children. Despite the high rate of HIV/AIDS infection, this means that Tanzania will see a population boom. In Poland, on the other hand, less than 17% of the population is under 15, so the number of women reaching childbearing age is much smaller. The average woman there has only 1.39 children, so the population of Poland will grow far less quickly than the other two countries, and may even go down.

9.

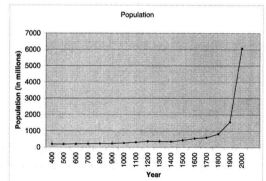

10. Answers will vary, depending on the migration students choose.

11. Answers will vary. Sample answers: cutting trees; planting crops; building houses, offices, factories, dams, roads, tunnels, and bridges.

12. Answers will vary. Sample answers: 1. petroleum—used to power vehicles, heat homes; 2. coal—used to create electricity, generate heat; 3. aluminum—used to make soda cans, car parts. Ways to conserve nonrenewable resources: recycle; use less; avoid wasteful packaging; develop new technologies that use less of these resources.

13. Answers will vary. Sample answers: 1. wind—used to generate electricity; 2. solar energy—used for heat, electricity; 3. water—used to generate electricity, run machinery

14. Answers will vary. Sample answer: Yes, it could happen again. In recent years, several diseases have threatened to become pandemics, including ebola in Africa, SARS in Asia and Canada, and

avian flu, which has spread to birds around the world and can be transmitted from birds to people; if the disease changes so it can be passed from person to person, it could be the next global pandemic.

15. 1. b; 2. d; 3. a; 4. c

16. 1. F; As well as location, the study of geography involves knowing about the characteristics of places (both physical and human), regions, movement, and how people interact with their environments. 2. T; 3. F; In geography, customs include many aspects of culture, including celebrations, ceremonies, religious observances, and more. 4. T; 5. T

17.

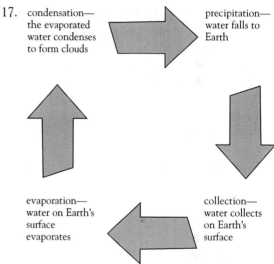

condensation—the evaporated water condenses to form clouds

precipitation—water falls to Earth

collection—water collects on Earth's surface

evaporation—water on Earth's surface evaporates

18. Answers will vary. Sample answers: 1. tall hardwood trees, such as mahogany and teak; vines, such as bougainvillea; epiphytes, such as orchids, bromeliads; shade-tolerant plants, such as ferns; 2. acacia trees, baobab trees, thornbushes, sturdy

grasses; 3. deciduous trees, such as oak, hickory, beech, hemlock, maple, basswood, cottonwood, elm, willow; spring-flowering herbs; 4. oak, olive trees, cedar, sagebrush, broom, eucalyptus; 5. deciduous trees, such as beech, oak, birch, hickory, pecan; ferns; mosses; 6. low-growing plants, such as mosses, heaths, lichens, sedges, liverworts, grasses; 7. ground-hugging shrubs and short woody trees, such as cactus, brittle bush, creosote bush, ironwood, Joshua trees, prickly pear, yucca; 8. conifers, such as fir, spruce, cedar, pine; deciduous trees, such as poplar, birch; 9. grasses, sagebrush

19. 1. front; 2. tornado; 3. drought; 4. precipitation; 5. climate

20. 1. c; 2. f; 3. a; 4. b; 5. g; 6. e; 7. d

21. 1. e; 2. b; 3. g; 4. d; 5. c; 6. a; 7. f

22. 1. What is the equator? 2. What is cardinal direction? 3. What is taiga? 4. What is a glacier? 5. What is a coral reef?

23.

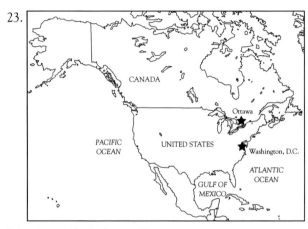

24. 1. c; 2. b; 3. d; 4. e; 5. a

25. Answers will vary. Sample answers: 1. Atlanta is northwest of Miami and southeast of Denver. 2. San Antonio is southwest of Houston and southeast of Phoenix. 3. Phoenix is southeast of Los Angeles and northwest of San Antonio. 4. San Francisco is northwest of Phoenix and southwest of Denver.

26.

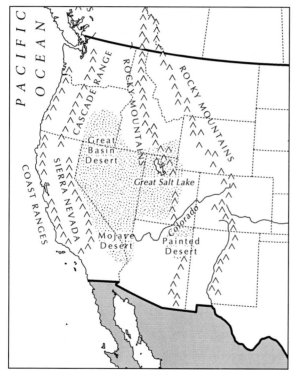

27. 1. f; 2. b; 3. c; 4. d; 5. i; 6. a; 7. e; 8. h; 9. g
28. Answers will vary. Sample answer: The government needs to know how many people live in each area so that it can make sure each state has the correct number of representatives for its population, and to make sure that federal, state, and local resources are allocated correctly.
29. Answers will vary.
30. Answers will vary. Sample answers: the introduction and spread of the automobile; the construction of the federal highway system; rapid post-war population growth caused by international immigration, movement of workers from farms to cities, and the baby boom; increase in available income; federal government policies that subsidized home ownership, including the GI Bill and mortgage-interest tax deduction; deterioration of living conditions in the cities, caused in part by the exodus of residents.
31. Answers will vary. Sample answers: High housing

costs in urban areas versus lower wages in outlying areas; high wages in urban areas combined with lower cost of living in outlying areas; the difference in lifestyle in a rural or smaller urban area as opposed to a major city.

32. Answers will vary.

33. Answers will vary. Sample answer: Most of the more affordable cities are in the midwestern states, including Ohio, Michigan, Illinois, and Wisconsin. Of the less affordable areas, all but one are in California. There are more employment opportunities in California than in, for example, Flint, Michigan. With more employment and better pay, housing and other costs rise.

34. 1. T; 2. F; The northernmost point in the continental United States is in Minnesota. 3. F; The United States and Canada are heavily industrialized, but there is still plenty of land used for farming. 4. T; 5. T

35. Answers will vary.

36. Answers will vary depending on where students live, but evacuation plans should include bringing a supply of any necessary medications, prescriptions in case refills are needed, important documents, a change of clothes, enough food and water to reach the intended destination, supplies, such as blankets, in case they get stranded along the way, and so forth.

37. Answers will vary. Sample answer:
Place: Las Vegas, Nevada
Changes: built a huge dam on the Colorado River, which created an artificial lake, the 157,900-acre Lake Mead; built a city in the middle of the desert; piped in water to create pools, fountains, lawns, and gardens in a desert area.

38. Tornado Alley, the region of the United States where tornadoes occur most frequently; it is centered on north Texas, Oklahoma, Kansas, Nebraska, and South Dakota.

39. 1. What is a megalopolis? 2. What is the

Tennessee Valley Authority (TVA)? 3. What is Lake Michigan? 4. What is urbanization? 5. What is Alaska?

40. 1. What is the St. Lawrence Seaway? 2. What is Vancouver? 3. What is Nunavut? 4. What is the Grand Banks area? 5. What is Quebec Province?

41.

42. 1. e; 2. b; 3. d; 4. a; 5. c

43. Answers will vary. Sample answers: 1. Buenos Aires is southeast of La Paz and southwest of Rio de Janeiro. 2. Lima is northwest of Sucre and southwest of Paramaribo. 3. Bogotá is southwest of Valencia and southeast of Medellín. 4. Quito is northwest of Lima and southwest of Paramaribo.

44.

45. 1. altiplano; 2. cordillera; 3. llano; 4. pampas; 5. sierra

46. 1. d; 2. c; 3. i; 4. b; 5. h; 6. j; 7. g; 8. a; 9. f; 10. e

47. 1. Cusco was the center of the Inca Empire. 2. Mazatlán is located on Mexico's Pacific coast. 3. Pereira is located on the Otun River. 4. In former times, when pirates were found in the Caribbean, this area on Puerto Rico's northwestern shore was used as a refuge by pirates. 5. The largest city in Brazil—indeed, in all South America—and an important port, São Paulo is Brazil's commercial, financial, and industrial center. 6. Taxco is one of the oldest mining sites in the Americas, with mines dating back to pre-Columbian times. 7. Ushuaia is located at the southernmost tip of Latin America.

48. Answers will vary. Sample answer:
Place: Mexico City, Mexico
Changes: filled in the system of lakes amid which the city was originally built to expand the city limits; built roads to connect the city with other areas

49. Answers may vary slightly.
Region 1: the Caribbean
Countries should include any three of the following: Antigua and Barbuda, Bahamas, Barbados, Cuba, Dominica, Dominican Republic, Grenada, Guadeloupe, Haiti, Jamaica, Martinique, Netherlands Antilles, Puerto Rico, St. Kitts and Nevis, St. Lucia, St. Vincent and the Grenadines, Trinidad and Tobago
Region 2: Mexico and Central America
Countries should include any three of the following: Belize, Costa Rica, El Salvador, Guatemala, Honduras, Mexico, Nicaragua, Panama
Region 3: South America
Countries should include any three of the following: Argentina, Bolivia, Brazil, Chile, Colombia, Ecuador, French Guiana, Guyana, Paraguay, Peru, Suriname, Uruguay, Venezuela

50.

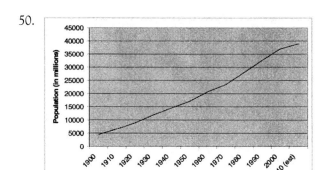

Population in 2020: Answers will vary. Sample answer: 42,000

51.
1811	Paraguay
1816	Argentina
1818	Chile
1819	Colombia
1821	Mexico
1821	Peru
1822	Brazil
1825	Bolivia
1828	Uruguay
1830	Venezuela
1830	Ecuador

Titles will vary.

52. 1. avocado; 2. chocolate; 3. coyote; 4. tomato

53. 1. f; 2. d; 3. e; 4. c; 5. a; 6. b

54. Answers may vary slightly. Sample answers: 1. Beggars can't be choosers. 2. Forewarned is forearmed. 3. If it isn't broken, don't fix it.

55. 1. T; 2. F; The countries of Latin America are very varied. 3. T; 4. T; 5. F; The primary language of Brazil is Portuguese.

Daily Warm-Ups: World Geography & Cultures

56.   1. What are the Andes? 2. What is the Amazon River? 3. What are pampas? 4. What is the Strait of Magellan?

57.

58.   1. b; 2. d; 3. a; 4. e; 5. c

59.   Answers will vary. Sample answers: 1. Berlin is southeast of Dublin and northeast of Madrid. 2. Lisbon is southwest of Madrid and Paris. 3. Rome is southeast of Paris and southwest of Helsinki. 4. Dublin is northwest of London and southwest of Oslo.

60.

61. Answers will vary. Sample answer: Iberia; Scandinavia; the Mediterranean; the British Isles; Benelux; the Alpine region
62. 1. c; 2. d; 3. g; 4. b; 5. a; 6. h; 7. i; 8. e; 9. f; 10. j
63. 1. Much of the North Sea's plentiful supply of crude oil flows through Aberdeen. 2. Trade, transportation, and distribution have always been an important part of Amsterdam's economy; many goods destined for mainland Europe go through Amsterdam. 3. The U.N.'s International Court of Justice is located in the Hague. 4. Milan is a center of the fashion industry. 5. Although only one hill can be seen today, the original city of Rome was built on seven hills: the Quirinal, Viminal, Esquiline, and Caelian hills, which are promontories of an ancient volcanic ridge, and the Palatine, Aventine, and Capitoline hills.
64. 1. b; 2. f; 3. a; 4. d; 5. c; 6. e
65. Answers will vary. Sample answer: More people are using public transportation, carpooling, walking, or using bicycles.
66. 1. U; 2. C; 3. R; 4. G; 5. G; 6. G; 7. U; 8. R; 9. G; 10. G; 11. C; 12. R; 13. G; 14. R; 15. C; 16. R; 17. G; 18. C
67. Answers will vary. Sample answer: Europe's geography encourages fragmentation by separating groups of people. Some areas are separated by water, such as the English Channel and the Irish Sea. Some are separated by mountains, such as the Pyrenees or the Alps. This landscape facilitated the development of separate languages.
68. Answers will vary. Sample answer:
Place: Folkestone, England, the Chunnel
Changes: constructed a 32-mile-long tunnel under the English Channel to provide rail service between France and the United Kingdom

Daily Warm-Ups: World Geography & Cultures

69.

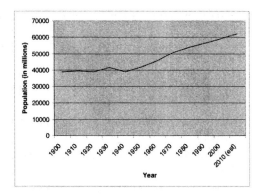

Answers will vary. Sample answer: The drops in population were probably due to World War I and World War II, both of which were fought extensively in France.

70. Most homes in Iceland use geothermal energy as a heat source.

71. 1. F; The Alps divide Italy from Europe. 2. T; 3. T; 4. F; There are a number of active volcanoes, especially in Italy and Iceland. 5. T

72. 1. What are the Alps? 2. What is Andorra? 3. What is the Chunnel (Channel Tunnel)? 4. What are fjords? 5. What is the North Sea?

73.

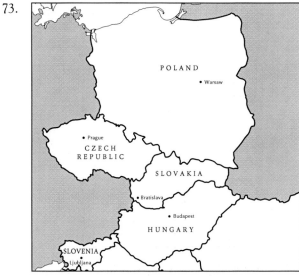

74. 1. e; 2. d; 3. a; 4. c; 5. b

75. Answers will vary. Sample answers:
1. Sofia is southeast of Sarajevo and southwest of Bucharest. 2. Tirane is southwest of Skopje and southeast of Zagreb. 3. Budapest is southeast of Bratislava and northwest of Sofia. 4. Zagreb is southwest of Budapest and northwest of Tirane.

76.

77. 1. Vistula; 2. Danube; 3. Balkan; 4. Yugoslavia; 5. Transylvania

78. Answers will vary. Sample answer: Under communism, workers in Eastern Europe were guaranteed jobs; in today's economy, a struggling business may lay off workers. Housing costs under communism were controlled; now rent is based on market factors. In many areas, old, inefficient factories find it difficult to compete in a broader market.

79. Answers will vary, depending on the country chosen.

80. 1. Dinaric Alps; 2. Transylvanian Alps; 3. Danube; 4. Balkan Peninsula; 5. North European Plain

81. 1. h; 2. g; 3. j; 4. e; 5. c; 6. f; 7. i; 8. b; 9. a; 10. d

82. 1. E; 2. H; 3. E; 4. H; 5. H

83. 1. Andrew; 2. John; 3. Joseph; 4. Christopher; 5. Mark; 6. Peter; 7. Paul; 8. Agnes; 9. Elizabeth; 10. Eva; 11. Catherine; 12. Christina; 13. Margaret; 14. Sophie

84. 1. O; 2. S; 3. S; 4. S; 5. S; 6. U; 7. U; 8. S; 9. S; 10. S; 11. S; 12. S; 13. S; 14. S

Daily Warm-Ups: World Geography & Cultures

85.

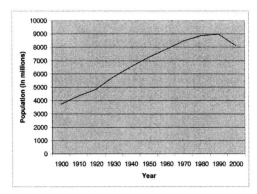

Answers will vary. Sample answer: The population of Bulgaria has been going down. This may be because, since the fall of the communist regime in 1990, Bulgarians are now able to emigrate in order to look for better opportunities elsewhere.

86. 1. F; Eastern Europe has a humid continental climate, unaffected by moderating sea breezes.
2. T; 3. T; 4. T; 5. F; The borders of countries in Eastern Europe changed radically in the late 1980s and early 1990s.

87. 1. What is Yugoslavia? 2. What is the Danube? 3. What are the Carpathian Mountains? 4. What is humid continental?

88.

89. 1. c; 2. d; 3. a; 4. e; 5. b
90. Answers will vary. Sample answers: 1. Minsk is southwest of Vilnius and northwest of Kiev. 2. Riga is northwest of Minsk and southwest of Tallinn. 3. Kiev is southeast of Minsk and southwest of Moscow. 4. Tallinn is northeast of Riga and northwest of Moscow.
91.

92. Answers will vary, depending on the country chosen.
93. 1. j; 2. b; 3. f; 4. h; 5. i; 6. a; 7. c; 8. g; 9. d; 10. e
94. 1. chernozem; 2. permafrost; 3. tundra; 4. taiga; 5. steppe
95. 1. Most of these cities lie in the westernmost part of the region; almost all are west of 65° E. 2. In this part of the region, the land is flatter and the climate is more temperate, making the area more conducive to farming and to other land uses that lead eventually to urbanization.
96. 1. e; 2. d; 3. b; 4. c; 5. a
97. Answers will vary. Sample answer: 1. my commute to my after-school job; 2. 3 miles; 3. 1,924 times; 4. 962 days, or more than two and a half years
98. Answers will vary. Sample answer: Russia's climate. Because Russia is so far north and has such a severe climate, its winters are long and cold. Neither Napoleon nor Hitler prepared the army for the brutal cold. Thousands of men froze

Daily Warm-Ups: World Geography & Cultures

102. 1. T; 2. F; Russia is by far the largest country in the area. 3. T; 4. T; 5. F; Russia has extensive natural resources.

103. 1. What is Russia? 2. What are the steppes? 3. What is the Black Sea? 4. What is Siberia?

104.

105. 1. b; 2. d; 3. e; 4. c; 5. a

106. Answers will vary. Sample answers: 1. Damascus is southwest of Tehran and northwest of Sanaa. 2. Tehran is northeast of Baghdad and southeast of Ankara. 3. Baghdad is northwest of Muscat and northeast of Amman. 4. Ankara is northwest of Tehran and Damascus.

107.

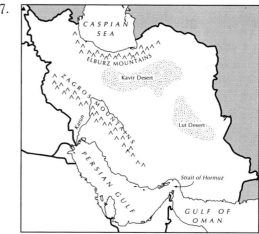

108. 1. profession of faith; 2. praying five times daily; 3. giving a percentage of income to charity; 4. fasting between sunup and sundown during the holy month of Ramadan; 5. for those who can afford to do so, making the *hajj*, or pilgrimage to

the holy city of Mecca, in Saudi Arabia
109. Answers will vary, depending on the country chosen.
110. 1. f; 2. g; 3. j; 4. c; 5. e; 6. a; 7. h; 8. d; 9. b; 10. i
111. 1. irrigation; 2. oasis; 3. wadi; 4. monsoon; 5. desert
112. Answers will vary, depending on the city chosen.
113. Answers will vary. A bar graph would be a good way to show this information.
114.

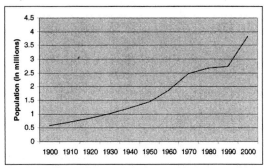

Answers will vary. Sample answer: 4,903 million

115. Answers will vary. Sample answers: kebabs, including doner (lamb or chicken sliced from a turning spit, usually served in pita bread with onions and tomatoes); shish (lamb, beef, or chicken grilled on wooden skewers); and kofte (meatballs, usually grilled). Pide is a long, thin bread topped with meat, vegetables, or cheese, then baked.

116. 1. T; 2. T; 3. F; Over the last century, boundaries and borders in this region have changed many times. 4. F; The region has long been torn by conflict between members of different religious groups. 5. T

117. Answers will vary. Sample answer: Some of these names describe the region as it relates to another region. Both "the Near East" and "the Middle East" describe the region from a Eurocentric perspective; it is "near" or "middle" in relation to Europe. The other name, "Southwest Asia," describes the region in terms of continent and

direction, not in terms of its relation to any other region.

118. 1. What is the Arabian Plateau? 2. What is Islam? 3. What are the Tigris and Euphrates? 4. What is oil (petroleum, crude oil)? 5. What is Israel?

119.

120. 1. c; 2. d; 3. e; 4. a; 5. b
121. Answers will vary. Sample answers: 1. Sudan is southeast of Libya and northwest of Ethiopia. 2. Ethiopia is southeast of Egypt and northeast of Uganda. 3. Nigeria is south of Niger and east of Benin. 4. Kenya is east of Uganda and south of Ethiopia.

122.

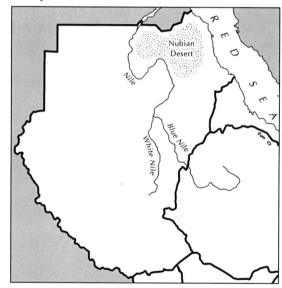

123. Answers will vary. Regions and countries could include the following:

Daily Warm-Ups: World Geography & Cultures

North Africa: Algeria, Egypt, Libya, Morocco, Tunisia, Western Sahara

West Africa: Benin, Burkina Faso, Cape Verde, Gambia, Ghana, Guinea, Guinea Bissau, Ivory Coast, Liberia, Mali, Mauritania, Niger, Nigeria, Senegal, Sierra Leone, Togo

Central Africa: Burundi, Cameroon, Central African Republic, Chad, Democratic Republic of the Congo, Equatorial Guinea, Gabon, Republic of the Congo, Rwanda, São Tomé and Principe

East Africa: Comoros, Djibouti, Eritrea, Ethiopia, Kenya, Madagascar, Seychelles, Somalia, Sudan, Uganda

Southern Africa: Angola, Botswana, Lesotho, Malawi, Mozambique, Namibia, South Africa, Swaziland, Tanzania, Zambia, Zimbabwe

124. Answers will vary. Sample answer:
The borders chosen by European colonial powers did not reflect ethnic divisions within regions. Some colonial boundaries divided members of one ethnic group. Some combined ethnic groups that had a history of conflict with one another. This continues to cause problems today because some African nations claim parts of other nations on the basis of ethnic groups. In other countries, conflict between ethnic groups has led to unrest and civil war.

125. 1. c; 2. e; 3. b; 4. d; 5. a; 6. c; 7. b; 8. c; 9. c; 10. e; 11. d; 12. c; 13. c; 14. b; 15. b; 16. d; 17. c; 18. b; 19. b; 20. b

126. The amount of water in the river varies dramatically from month to month, with the lowest months being January to June, and the highest months being August and September. The extreme increase in the amount of water being carried in those months would probably lead to regular flooding of the region near the river.

127. Answers will vary, depending on the country chosen.

128. 1. a; 2. e; 3. h; 4. c; 5. g; 6. b; 7. j; 8. i; 9. f; 10. d

129. 1. Almost all the cities listed are either on the coast or on a river. 2. Overland transportation in most parts of Africa is difficult. Thus, cities tended to arise in areas where the ocean or rivers made transportation easier.

130. Answers will vary.

131.

City	Population	Area (sq. mi.)	Population density per sq. mi.
Abidjan, Ivory Coast	3,300,000	115	28,700
Cairo, Egypt	12,200,000	500	24,400
Conakry, Guinea	1,300,000	62	21,000
Khartoum, Sudan	4,000,000	225	17,800
Kinshasa, Democratic Republic of the Congo	5,000,000	181	27,600
Nairobi, Kenya	2,000,000	90	22,200

132. Answers will vary. Sample answer:
Place: Nile River, Egypt
Changes: built a dam on the river at Aswan to control the annual flooding of the Nile; flooded a huge area to create an artificial lake, Lake Nasser; relocated thousands of residents of the area; covered ancient temples and other archaeological

areas with water; the end of the flooding means the land near the river no longer receives an annual coating of nutrient-rich silt carried by the water, forcing farmers to use artificial fertilizers; the decreased turbulence of the river has led to an increase in the parasitic disease schistosomiasis.

133.

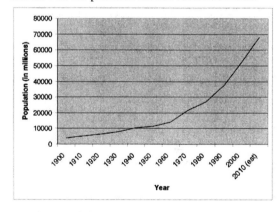

Population of the Democratic Republic of the Congo in 2020: Answers will vary. Sample answer:

87,007 million

134. 1. T; 2. F; The equator passes through the middle of Africa; countries on the equator include Gabon, the Republic of the Congo, the Democratic Republic of the Congo, Uganda, Kenya, and Somalia. 3. T; 4. F; Eritrea was part of Ethiopia until 1991, when it gained independence after a 30-year struggle. 5. T

135. 1. What is the Sahara Desert? 2. What is the Nile River? 3. What is Western Sahara? 4. What is Algeria? 5. What is desertification?

136. 1. What is the Sahel? 2. What is deforestation? 3. What is the Congo River? 4. What is cacao? 5. What is Nigeria?

137.

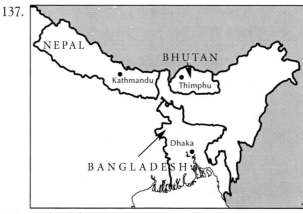

138. 1. b; 2. d; 3. e; 4. c; 5. a

139. Answers will vary. Sample answers: 1. Bangalore is northwest of Colombo and southwest of Calcutta. 2. Karachi is southwest of Islamabad and northwest of Calcutta. 3. Dhaka is northeast of Bangalore and southeast of Kathmandu. 4. Kabul is northwest of New Delhi and northeast of Karachi.

140.
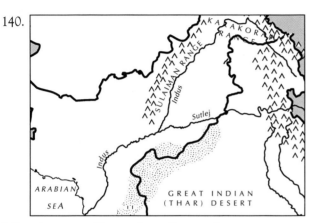

141. Answers will vary, depending on the country chosen.
142. 1. d; 2. b; 3. g; 4. f; 5. e; 6. c; 7. a
143. Answers will vary.
144. 1. Mumbai; 2. San Jose has about one fifth of the population density of the least densely populated city on the graph, Jakarta, and one thirteenth of the population density of the most densely populated city on the graph, Mumbai. 3. Answers will vary. Sample answer: advantages—would probably be ethnically and economically diverse; disadvantages—availability of adequate services such as sanitation, housing, healthcare, education; increased risk of spread of contagion due to crowded quarters.

145.
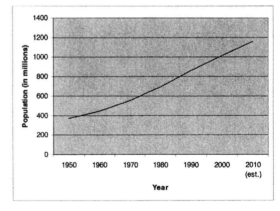

146. Answers will vary. Sample answers: samosas (deep-fried, triangular pastries filled with vegetables); bhaja (round vegetable fritters); pakora (round fritters made of flour and vegetables); puri (disks of deep-fried dough); idli (fermented rice cakes); dosa (crepes of lentil puree and fermented rice flour); lassi (yogurt drinks, either sweet or savory); chai (spiced tea)

147. Answers will vary. Sample answer: India's history and geography contribute to the multitude of languages. Geographically, the subcontinent is divided into several distinct sections, which encouraged the development of separate, distinct cultures. Over the centuries, many separate states developed. At different times, one state might conquer one or more other states, but the large empires that developed there rarely lasted. This geographic and cultural separation led to the development of a number of distinct languages, which are still found in India today.

148. 1. T; 2. F; In most of South Asia, the climate is hot and dry for half of the year, and hot and wet for the other half. 3. T; 4. T; 5. T

149. 1. What are the Himalayas? 2. What is the monsoon? 3. What is India? 4. What is Pakistan? 5. What is Sri Lanka?

150.

151. 1. b; 2. e; 3. d; 4. a; 5. c
152. Answers will vary. Sample answers: 1. Bangkok is southeast of Yangon and southwest of Hanoi. 2. Hong Kong is northeast of Hanoi and southwest of Taipei. 3. Seoul is southeast of Pyongyang and northwest of Tokyo. 4. Tokyo is northeast of Hanoi and Beijing.
153.

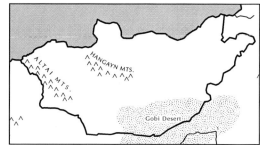

Bonus: Russia is to the north, China is to the south.
154. Answers will vary, depending on the country chosen.
155. 1. d; 2. b; 3. h; 4. j; 5. i; 6. k; 7. e; 8. f; 9. g; 10. a; 11. c

156. 1. loess; 2. paddy; 3. Ring of Fire; 4. volcano; 5. monsoon
157. Answers will vary. Sample answer: In some parts of China, severe floods have been blamed on deforestation caused by cutting down trees. The passage says that people in China throw away more than 45 billion pairs of chopsticks every year. That many chopsticks require cutting down a lot of trees. If people in China keep using disposable chopsticks, more and more areas will lose all their trees, which could have significant environmental effects. Also, all those chopsticks create a challenge for waste disposal. Wooden chopsticks can't be recycled, so they all end up in landfills. That many chopsticks take up a lot of space.
158. 1. Manila; 2. Hong Kong; 3. Answers will vary. Sample answer: Hong Kong is an island, so it is difficult for the population to spread out.
159. Sitting above four tectonic plates, Japan is one of the world's most earthquake-prone countries.

Japanese building requirements call for buildings that can withstand severe earthquakes. In 1995, an earthquake in Kobe killed about 6,400 people. Some buildings that were believed to be earthquake-safe collapsed in that quake. If a building does not have enough steel reinforcing bars, or if the bars are too weak, the building may not be able to withstand the force of an earthquake.

160. Answers will vary. Sample answer:
Place: Three Gorges Dam, China
Changes: flooded 395 square miles of land and built a dam one and a half miles wide, displacing 1.2 million people, in order to enable 10,000-ton ships to sail into the nation's interior, generate electricity, and control flooding of the Yangtze River

161. Answers will vary. Sample answer:
Region 1: Northeast China; boundaries: Amur River, North China Plain, Greater Khingan Range; the core of the earliest Chinese civilization; still China's industrial and administrative center
Region 2: Southeast China; boundaries: North China Plain, South China Sea, western highlands; rich soil and mild climate make it an agricultural center

162. Answers will vary. Sample answers: tea, fried rice, grilled rice balls, noodles, dumplings, soup

163.

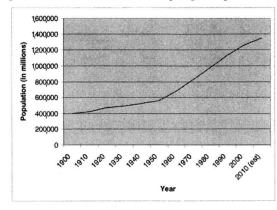

Answer Key

Answers will vary. Sample answer: No, the policy does not seem to be working, as China's population has increased by more than 200 million people since the policy was introduced.

164. 1. T; 2. F; Japan often experiences violent typhoons. 3. T; 4. F; The governments and economies of the two countries are very different. 5. T

165. 1. What is China? 2. What is Hong Kong? 3. What is an earthquake? 4. What is rice? 5. What is soy?

166.

167. 1. b; 2. d; 3. c; 4. a

168. Answers will vary. Samp[le] southeast of Perth and northwest o[f] 2. Canberra is northwest of Wellington and southeast of Perth. 3. Nouméa is northeast of Canberra and northwest of Wellington. 4. Wellington is southeast of Canberra and northeast of Dunedin.

169.

. Answers will vary, depending on the country chosen.

171. 1. c; 2. b; 3. f; 4. i; 5. a; 6. j; 7. g; 8. d; 9. e; 10. h

172. 1. coral reef; 2. atoll; 3. archipelago; 4. cyclone; 5. tsunami

173. 1. c; 2. c; 3. a; 4. c; 5. a; 6. b; 7. a

174. If global warming causes sea levels to rise, this tiny, low-lying island nation could be completely washed away.

175. Answers will vary. Actual nicknames for these cities: Adelaide—City of Churches; Auckland—City of Sails; Brisbane—The River City; Nouméa—Paris of the Pacific; Perth—City of Lights; Sydney—The Harbour City; Te Puke—Kiwifruit Capital of the World

176.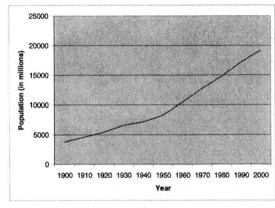

Answers will vary. Sample answer: 20,971 million

177. 1. Most of these cities lie on or near Australia's coasts; none are located in the country's interior. 2. Much of interior Australia is desert. The little rainfall the country receives falls near the coasts, especially the eastern coast. For this reason, most of Australia's cities are located along the coast.

178. 1. F; Australia and New Zealand were British

colonies until 1901. 2. T; 3. T; 4. T; 5. F; On many
Pacific islands, the soil is thin and often depleted;
most islands grow only enough food for their own
needs.

179. Answers will vary. Sample answer: Australia is
      geographically isolated. This means that plants
      and animals developed here with no outside
      influences.

180. 1. Who are the Maori? 2. What is the
      International Date Line? 3. What is phosphate?
      4. What is Antarctica? 5. What is an atoll?

Turn downtime into learning time!

For information on other titles in the

Daily *Warm-Ups* series,

visit our web site: walch.com

ures